# THE HIDDEN BUSINESS VALUE

## Business and economic value created by business support services

### Abstract

Business organizations compete for the best sustainable competitive advantage in a world that is changing quickly and dramatically due to the new economy driven by the information age. Do businesses, in the quest for the sustainable competitive advantage, use all available resources to their benefit? Data, information, and knowledge are a sustainable source of competitive advantage generated from within their own business support services. What is economic value and how can it be measured? Are the Romanian business organizations ready to switch their business philosophy to the new economy driven by the information age?

Marius Daraban, PhD

# Table of Contents

# 1 Research scope

The main scope of the research is an assessment of the perception of economic value creation of business organizations through their business support services.

The research was developed by TopCFO and was included in a Ph.D. research with the topic of economic/business value creation by business support services.

# 2 Questionnaire description

The questionnaire was available over social network contacts from 14.11.2017 until 30.12.2017. Over the time where data have been collected, about 7 weeks, based on the voluntary contribution of respondents there have been **93** answers recorded from business professionals and executives.

The questionnaire parameters and items are presented below:

## 2.1 Target group: Support activities responsible (as per value chain concept)

Equivalent corporate functions or similar:

CEO, CFO, Legal Manager, Finance Manager, Head of Controlling, Head of Accounting, HR Manager, IT, Procurement Manager, sales and marketing manager, logistic manager, operation and production manager, quality assurance and control manager

## 2.2 Objective

- Feedback from the business environment regarding the scope of the Ph.D. Thesis, support activities generate value and contribute to the value chain of the business.
- Is the Romanian business environment ready for the switch to value and knowledge-based economy, the 21$^{st}$-century business model?

## 2.3 Output

Assessment of perception of economic/business value creation, value and knowledge management. Assessment of value creation perception through business support services

## 2.4 Used infrastructure

For the data collection, presentation and recording, free web application provided by Google Inc. have been used. The used applications have been Google Forms, Google Sites and Google Sheets.

The link to the website for data collection: https://sites.google.com/dmc.ro/mariusdaraban

The website was created for research purposes, no confidential or other data has been collected through web cookies, scripts and similar.

The languages used for the data collection questionnaires have been English, German and Romanian.

## 2.5   Questionnaire items

1. Size of business
    a. Small (1-100 employees)
    b. Medium (101-1000 employees)
    c. Big (corporation) (1001 - employees)
2. Majority shareholder
    a. Foreign
    b. Romanian
3. Business type
    a. Product business type
    b. Services business type
    c. Product and services business type
4. Your role in your organization
    a. CEO
    b. CFO / Finance Manager
    c. Head of Controlling or Head of Accounting
    d. HR Manager
    e. IT Manager
    f. Procurement Manager
    g. Sales, Commercial or Marketing Manager
    h. Operations or Production Manager
    i. Quality Manager
    j. Logistics Manager or similar
5. The information age has transformed/changed the way things are done in my area of responsibility
6. IT&C is omnipresent in my area of responsibility

7. I expect that future developments in information technology and communication will change and transform even more the way of operating in my area of responsibility
8. Business value/business process value is a common concept in my area of responsibility
9. Value-based management is the common management style in my area of responsibility
10. Value stream and value stream mapping is a common concept in my area of responsibility
11. The vision, mission, and values of my area of responsibility support the value creation process through equity maximization
12. Knowledge management learning and development plans are common concepts in my area of responsibility
13. Knowledge is created, stored and shared in my area of responsibility
14. Knowledge management tools, processes, and procedures are used in my area of responsibility
15. Business support activities (indirect productive activities) contribute to the business value creation process
16. The value created by indirect productive activities created value is monitored and measured
17. The following business support services are creating value and are important for my area of responsibility [Financial Accounting]

18. The following business support services are creating value and are important for my area of responsibility [Management Accounting]
19. The following business support services are creating value and are important for my area of responsibility [Legal Services]
20. The following business support services are creating value and are important for my area of responsibility [HR Management]
21. The following business support services are creating value and are important for my area of responsibility [IT&C Management]
22. The following business support services are creating value and are important for my area of responsibility [Procurement]
23. Please rate the value contribution to your business value chain of the following business support services (1 - no value contribution, 5 - maximal value contribution) [Financial Accounting]
24. Please rate the value contribution to your business value chain of the following business support services (1 - no value contribution, 5 - maximal value contribution) [Management Accounting]
25. Please rate the value contribution to your business value chain of the following business support services (1 - no value contribution, 5 - maximal value contribution) [Legal Services]
26. Please rate the value contribution to your business value chain of the following business support

services (1 - no value contribution, 5 - maximal value contribution) [HR Management]

27. Please rate the value contribution to your business value chain of the following business support services (1 - no value contribution, 5 - maximal value contribution) [IT&C Management]

28. Please rate the value contribution to your business value chain of the following business support services (1 - no value contribution, 5 - maximal value contribution) [Procurement]

29. Do you use value-based performance evaluation tools like [ Economic Value Added (EVA)]?

30. Do you use value-based performance evaluation tools like [Cash Value Added (CVA)]?

31. Do you use value-based performance evaluation tools like [Economic Profit (EP)]?

32. I am interested to find out more about ... [business value]

33. I am interested to find out more about ... [value-based management]

34. I am interested to find out more about ... [Value based KPI's]

35. To receive the final report please enter your email below

## 2.6 Post data collection

On 30.12.2017 the data collection process was closed, and the homepage of the website used for data collection was updated accordingly.

The 93 recorded answers are based on the professional experience and seniority of the respondents as senior business professionals and executives of active operating business organizations.

For the evaluation of the multiple options received answers the following quantifications have been used.

## 2.7 Questionnaire scale used

For the quantification of the opinion of the respondent the following scales have

| | | | |
|---|---|---|---|
| strongly disagree | 1 | Yes | 3 |
| disagree | 2 | Maybe | 2 |
| neutral | 3 | No | 1 |
| agree | 4 | been used: | |
| strongly agree | 5 | | |

# 3 Questionnaire answers

The questionnaire raised some interest with the respondents. The timeframe the data collection was open was the end of 2017 (14.11.2017-30.12.2017).

The questionnaire answers came from people with extensive work experience that held senior management positions at the company where they work.

The respondents have a deep and thorough understanding of their business and business processes, therefore, being able to understand and asses the questionnaire items to their full extent.

The questionnaire items are grouped and asses the following topics:

## 3.1 Generic description of the respondent's business and company (items 1 – 4)

In terms of *business size*, the opinions are well represented as they come from all business sizes, corporations and medium business organizations have 40% each whereas small business organizations have the remaining 20% of the expressed opinions. This balanced weighting shows that the items of the questionnaire are relevant and important for all business sizes.

The *majority shareholder* can have a big influence on the definition and acceptance of value-driven business management. More than 70% of the respondents have a foreign shareholder and have value management included in their management principles and philosophy. The high interest is determined by mother-companies of the Romanian operations, that are coming from more developed markets where the value creation and value management is more present.

The *business type* weighting shows that value management is not an issue that is business type-specific, it is a constant of the management principles of the 21$^{st}$ century modern and efficient business organization.

The most interest was raised at the executive level of the business organizations. The CEO + CFO share of the opinions represent more than 50%. If we consider the extended executive team, including the HR + Sales-, Commercial-, or Marketing Manager share of expressed opinions the interest rate jumps at 80%.

It can be concluded that value management and value creation is a topic of the concerns most senior and executive management. In the case of CEO and CFO, the high acceptance and interest of value and value management can be traced back to the proximity to the shareholders, the mentioned corporate senior executive roles are compensated through management contracts that have a bonus criteria's that depend and target the created business value.

**Item 4 - Your role in your organization**

## 3.2 Perception and acceptance of IT induced changes (items 5-7)

IT&C as a change agent has a clear recognition, presence, and influence over the "classical" way of doing business with more than 90% of the expressed opinions. Also, there is no doubt that IT&C will continue to change the way business is done, more than 95% of expressed opinion sustains this fact.

The information revolution and the resulting change and transformation process of all "classical" concepts have begun in the 1990s. Today, almost 30 years later, the once cutting edge, visionary and sometimes sci-fi looking breakthroughs in IT&C have established themselves and drive and continue the change and transformation process of the "classical" way of doing business.

When considering the perception of the impact of IT induced changes the conclusion is clear, IT is here to stay. More than 90% of the respondents have indicated that the changes determined by IT are recognized and will be even more present in the next future.

When considering the "small companies – companies with turnover <1MEUR "the perception of IT and IT induced changes are more than 95% of respondents.

The "mid-sized companies" score "only a 90% acceptance at this item.

The "corporations" align themselves with a score of 90% but has still some opinions that do not agree and accept the IT induced changes.

## 3.3 Perception and acceptance of value-based management (items 8 – 11)

In most business organizations the concept of business value, business process value is a common concept (71%). About 30% of the business organizations are still not adopters of the concepts, being not yet ready to embrace the challenges of the "new economy", information, data, and knowledge-driven economy.

About 75% of the expressed opinions have indicated the adoption of value-based management as a management style, that sustains and supports the adoption of business value and business process value from the previous item. There are still about 25% of the respondents that are not ready for the value-based management philosophy.

The adopters of value-based management and the corresponding business value concepts are using also value stream and value stream mapping as management tools in their business organizations.

The adoption of value concepts and value-based management is applied and used also for the support of strategic management concepts like vision, mission, and values.

## Responses according to Business size

- small companies

~73% consider business value/business process value as being common in their area of responsibility

~78% are having value-based management as their common management style

~53% are using and tracking value through value stream mapping

~99.6% are recognizing that the vision, mission, and values of their company are supporting the value creation process through shareholder equity maximization

- mid-size companies

~70% consider business value/business process value as common in their area of responsibility

~72% are having value-based management as their common management style

~70% are using and tracking value through value stream mapping

~80% are recognizing that the vision, mission, and values of their company are supporting the value creation process through shareholder equity maximization

- corporations

~70% consider business value/business process value as common in their area of responsibility

~85% are having value-based management as their common management style

~70% are using and tracking value through value stream mapping

~70% are recognizing that the vision, mission, and values of their company are supporting the value creation process through shareholder equity maximization

Business size seems to be an aspect that is influencing and determining the acceptance and the perception of value-based management.

Small companies tend to have a much higher acceptance of the core value-based management concepts on almost all items than other company sizes.

Corporations have the lowest perception and acceptance, only 70%, when considering the vision, mission and values as a support of the value creation process through shareholder value maximization. This can partly be explained by the greatest "distance" from the shareholder in corporations whereas in small and mid-sized companies the proximity to the shareholder is an influencing factor.

Corporations nowadays tend to be driven more by executive benefits and business politics rather than to be driven by the core principles of value-based management.

It is interesting to extrapolate and to anticipate the evolution of this aspect in corporations when considering the increasing influence and disruption of IT&C through machine learning, artificial intelligence, big data, etc.

## 3.4 Perception and acceptance of knowledge and knowledge management (items12-14)

Knowledge management, learning, and development plans are common concepts for more than 90% of the respondents that indicate that knowledge is created, stored and shared by their business organizations through the usage of proper and adequate knowledge management tools, processes and procedures.

**Responses according to Business size**

- small companies

~95% of the respondents accept that knowledge management, learning, and development plans are common concepts

~84% of the respondents accept that knowledge is created, stored and shared in their area of responsibility

~95% of the respondents accept that knowledge management tools and processes are used in their area of responsibility

- mid-sized companies

~95% of the respondents accept that knowledge management, learning, and development plans are common concepts

~84% of the respondents accept that knowledge is created, stored and shared in their area of responsibility

~97% of the respondents accept that knowledge management tools and processes are used in their area of responsibility

- corporations

~84% of the respondents accept that knowledge management, learning, and development plans are common concepts

~78% of the respondents accept that knowledge is created, stored and shared in their area of responsibility

~81% of the respondents accept that knowledge management tools and processes are used in their area of responsibility

Corporations are scoring the lowest score at the perception and acceptance of knowledge and knowledge management. Generally, corporations tend to have a quite strict and comprehensive set of rules and procedures on what employees are expected to do and that covers mainly the operational aspects of the activity. Knowledge management and knowledge are mainly a high-level topic that is supposed to be on the activity list of the modern business manager and executive.

*Can this mean that Romanian operating businesses are not interested very much in the creation, storage, and dissemination of knowledge? Due to the anonymity of the responses, the exact answer cannot be given, a hint can be given when looking at the responses according to the nationality of the majority shareholder.*

## Responses according to the nationality of majority shareholder

- Romanian majority shareholder

~88% of the respondents accept that knowledge management, learning, and development plans are common concepts

~77% of the respondents accept that knowledge is created, stored and shared in their area of responsibility

~76% of the respondents accept that knowledge management tools and processes are used in their area of responsibility

- Foreign majority shareholder

~92% of the respondents accept that knowledge management, learning, and development plans are common concepts

~85% of the respondents accept that knowledge is created, stored and shared in their area of responsibility

~90% of the respondents accept that knowledge management tools and processes are used in their area of responsibility

Romanian majority shareholder companies tend to have a considerably lower acceptance and perception of knowledge and knowledge management indicating that Romanian companies are still driven mainly by the "industrial age" management style and do not accept not perceive the value of Knowledge and knowledge to their full potential.

## 3.5 Generic perception and monitoring of business support activities as business value contributor (items 15-16)

Business support activities, one of the most information, data, and knowledge-intensive business activities are perceived as being a value contributor to the business organization process with more than 95% of the opinions.

The value creation of business support activities is considered as monitored only by 65% that is a considerable drop from the acknowledgment of the value contribution, from 95% to 65%.

More than 35% do not consider or do not monitor the created value of indirect productive activities due to no involvement in the financial result of the business organization.

The diminished perception can indicate that still, a considerable part of the business organizations is purely financially driven, no value creation aspects or shareholder value creation aspects are considered. One argument in favor of this reduced perception is that the Romanian operations are considered only an extended workbench" or a market share for their mother companies that have direct proximity to shareholder value creation.

### Responses according to Business size

- small companies

~88% of the respondents accept that business support activities (indirect productive activities) contribute to the business value creation process

~36% of the respondents accept that the value created by indirect productive activities is monitored and measured

- mid-sized companies

~99.8% of the respondents accept that business support activities (indirect productive activities) contribute to the business value creation process

~75% of the respondents accept that the value created by indirect productive activities is monitored and measured

- corporations

~97% of the respondents accept that business support activities (indirect productive activities) contribute to the business value creation process

~68% of the respondents accept that the value created by indirect productive activities is monitored and measured

Mid-sized companies are scoring the highest score at the perception and monitoring of the business support activities as business value contributors. One defining trait of mid-sized companies is that the company is well established and is setting additional ambitious goals for growth and development and for this it is looking at every possible usable and exploitable resource.

## 3.6 Specific perception of business support services assessment as a value creator and business importance and assessment of business support services created value (items 17- 28)

### 3.6.1 Financial accounting

**Financial accounting** is indicated as being a value creator only by 31% of the respondents that strongly agree with this fact. About 50% of the expressed opinions only agree with the value creation aspect of financial accounting.

This might be explained by the factual orientation of the statutory financial accounting system, which in Romania is mainly tax oriented and that does not or very little provide information that can be used for business management. Financial statutory accounting, especially in the case of Romania, is tax oriented and has very little or no impact in the business management process and is perceived mainly as a "burden" where the "classical bean-counter" role is predominant.

The perceived created value of financial accounting is considered as maximal value only by 22% scoring an average perceived value of 3.59 out of 5.0. The relatively low score indicates and sustains again the perceived role and of the financial statutory Romanian accounting system that lacks in support of business management information.

The perception and acceptance of financial accounting differ greatly when considering company size and nationality of the majority shareholder.

**Responses according to Business size**

- small companies

~63% of respondents strongly agree and agree to the fact that financial accounting is creating value for their business, financial accounting is scoring an average of 3.11 out of 5

- mid-size companies

~84% of respondents strongly agree and agree to the fact that financial accounting is creating value for their business, financial accounting is scoring an average of 3.75 out of 5

- corporations

~80% of respondents strongly agree and agree to the fact that financial accounting is creating value for their business, financial accounting is scoring an average of 3.68 out of 5

Small companies are more preoccupied with operational and daily activities and do not perceive financial accounting as real business support, whereas mid-size companies and corporations are more concerned about the flow and allocation of financial resources.

## Responses according to the nationality of majority shareholder

- Romanian

~70% of respondents strongly agree and agree to the fact that financial accounting is creating value for their business, financial accounting is scoring an average of 3.26 out of 5

- Foreign

~80% of respondents strongly agree and agree to the fact that financial accounting is creating value for their business, financial accounting is scoring an average of 3.73 out of 5

The Romanian companies tend to look at financial accounting more like a burden due to the excessively bureaucratic and tax-oriented Romanian financial accounting system.

Foreign companies tend to approach financial accounting more from the perspective of mandatory activity that has to be taken seriously when acting in a certain market.

### 3.6.2 Management accounting

**Management accounting** is indicated as being a business value creator by 43% that strongly agree, +12 % more than financial accounting. The combined opinions that strongly agree and agree to the management accounting as a business value creator role are 82% is somehow like the financial accounting combined opinions.

They perceive value contribution to the business value chain of management accounting is indicated as being maximal by 41% of the opinions. The combined opinions, 5 and 4, regarding perceive created value is indicated by 71% of the opinions. Management accounting average perceived value is 3.82 out of 5.0

**Responses according to Business size**

- small companies

~73% of respondents strongly agree and agree to the fact that management accounting is creating value for their business, management accounting is scoring an average of 2.89 out of 5

- mid-size companies

~83% of respondents strongly agree and agree to the fact that management accounting is creating value for their business, management accounting is scoring an average of 4.13 out of 5

- corporations

~85% of respondents strongly agree and agree to the fact that management accounting is creating value for their business, management accounting is scoring an average of 4.00 out of 5

Small companies tend not to regard management accounting as a decision process data provider. The full potential of management accounting is not perceived nor accepted considering their business stage of development.

## Responses according to the nationality of majority shareholder

- Romanian

~77% of respondents strongly agree and agree to the fact that management accounting is creating value for their business, management accounting is scoring an average of 3.33 out of 5

- Foreign

~80% of respondents strongly agree and agree to the fact that management accounting is creating value for their business, management accounting is scoring an average of 4.03 out of 5

The perception and acceptance of management accounting are slightly lower in Romanian companies as compared with foreign companies. The big difference is in the perceived created value by management accounting where foreign companies score 4.03 compared to the Romanian companies with only 3.33.

### 3.6.3   Legal services

**Legal services** are perceived as value creator only by 23% that strongly agree with this role. The combined opinions of strongly agree and agree for legal services as value creator is indicated by 65% of the respondents.

The perceived created value by legal services is rated as maximal by 18% and scores an average perceived created value score of 3.45 out of 5.0.

**Responses according to Business size**

- small companies

~42% of respondents strongly agree and agree to the fact that legal services are creating value for their business, legal services are scoring an average of 2.79 out of 5

- mid-size companies

~70% of respondents strongly agree and agree to the fact that legal services are creating value for their business, legal services are scoring an average of 3.65 out of 5 corporations

- corporations

~71% of respondents strongly agree and agree to the fact that legal services are creating value for their business, legal services are scoring an average of 3.59 out of 5

**Responses according to the nationality of majority shareholder**

- Romanian

~51% of respondents strongly agree and agree to the fact that legal services are creating value for their business, legal services are scoring an average of 3.11 out of 5

- Foreign

~70% of respondents strongly agree and agree to the fact that legal services are creating value for their business, legal services are scoring an average of 3.59 out of 5

For mid-sized companies and corporations, legal services are getting an important share of the company's attention due to its complex and widespread business operations. The score awarded is average 3,65 for mid-size companies and 3.59 for corporations.

The responses according to the nationality of majority shareholder differ greatly, Romanian companies perceive only 51% that legal services are creating value and are important for their business, whereas Foreign companies perceive 70% that legal services are creating value and are important for their business. The average score also differs widely, Romanian companies score legal services at 3.11 whereas Foreign companies score legal services at 3.59.

### 3.6.4   Human resource management

**Human Resources** Management is considered as being a value creator by 50% that strongly agree. More than 85% of the respondents consider HR as a business value creator.

The created value contribution of 4 and 5 by HRM is indicated by 82% of the expressed opinions. HRM is scoring an average perceived created value score of 4.18 out of 5.0

This relatively high score is explained by proximity to the operational part of the business management and influences the entire business.

In the case of Human Resources, there are no significant changes and differences in perceived importance and value contribution when looking at the size of the company and at the nationality of the majority shareholder.

### 3.6.5  IT&C Management

**IT&C Management** is considered as a value creator by 58% of the opinions that strongly agree with this role. The combined value creator perception is indicated by about 90% of the opinions.

The perceived value contribution to the business value creation process is rated as maximal by 46% of the expressed opinions scoring an average perceived created value of 4.27 out of 5.0. The average perceived created value is the highest of the assessed business support services and can be explained by the massive presence in daily business operations.

**Responses according to Business size**

- small companies

~79% of respondents strongly agree and agree to the fact that IT&C Management is creating value for their business, IT&C Management is scoring an average of 3.84 out of 5

- mid-size companies

~94% of respondents strongly agree and agree to the fact that IT&C Management is creating value for their business, IT&C Management is scoring an average of 4.40 out of 5

- corporations

~88% of respondents strongly agree and agree to the fact that IT&C Management is creating value for their business, IT&C Management is scoring an average of 4.29 out of 5

## Responses according to nationality of majority shareholder

- Romanian

~82% of respondents strongly agree and agree to the fact that IT&C Management is creating value for their business, IT&C Management is scoring an average of 3.89 out of 5

- Foreign

~93% of respondents strongly agree and agree to the fact that IT&C Management is creating value for their business, IT&C Management is scoring an average of 4.39 out of 5

### 3.6.6 Procurement

**Procurement** is considered as a business value creator only by 33% of the expressed opinions and summing up about 70% of the opinions that strongly agree and agree.

The perceived created value of Procurement is rated as maximal only by about 30% of the opinions. Procurement is scoring 3.77 out of 5.0 in the average perceived created value.

**<u>Responses according to Business size</u>**

- small companies

~57% of respondents strongly agree and agree to the fact that Procurement is creating value for their business, Procurement is scoring an average of 3.11 out of 5

- mid-size companies

~79% of respondents strongly agree and agree to the fact that Procurement is creating value for their business, Procurement is scoring an average of 3.95 out of 5

- corporations

~69% of respondents strongly agree and agree to the fact that Procurement is creating value for their business, Procurement is scoring an average of 3.94 out of 5

**Responses according to the nationality of majority shareholder**

- Romanian

~70% of respondents strongly agree and agree to the fact that Procurement is creating value for their business, Procurement is scoring an average of 3.48 out of 5

- Foreign

~70% of respondents strongly agree and agree to the fact that Procurement is creating value for their business, Procurement is scoring an average of 3.89 out of 5

## 3.7 Usage assessment of value-driven performance indicators (items 29-31)

EVA is used by 46% of the respondents, CVA scores 40% and EP about 50%. This similar value indicates that about 50% still not use a clearly documented and known concept to evaluate their business performance.

**Responses according to Business size**

- small companies

~63% of respondents **do not use** EVA, CVA or EP

- mid-size companies

~35% of respondents **do not use** EVA or EP

~48% of respondents **do not use** CVA

- corporations

~35% of respondents **do not use** EVA, CVA or EP

**Responses according to the nationality of majority shareholder**

- Romanian

~55% of respondents **do not use** EVA, CVA or EP

- Foreign

~35% of respondents **do not use** EVA, CVA or EP

## 3.8 Interest assessment for business value, value-based management and value-driven KPI's (items 32-34)

Between 70% and 80% of the opinions indicate that there is a clear and decisive uncovered demand for more information and data about business value, value-based management, and value-driven KPI's.

## Responses according to Business size

- small companies

~70% of respondents are interested to find out more about business value, value-based management or value-based KPI's

- mid-size companies

~74% of respondents are interested to find out more about business value, value-based management or value-based KPI's

- corporations

~80% of respondents are interested to find out more about business value, value-based management or value-based KPI's

## Responses according to nationality of majority shareholder

- Romanian

~80% of respondents are interested to find out more about business value, value-based management or value-based KPI's

- Foreign

~75% of respondents are interested to find out more about business value, value-based management or value-based KPI's

# 4   Final conclusions

The data provided by the questionnaire is not representative from the statistical point of view for the Romanian business environment but due to the heterogeneous nature of businesses in terms of location, size, type, and majority shareholders give an indication readiness of the Romanian economy for the challenges and opportunities of the information age, the age where data, information and knowledge has become the prime commodity.

The globalization puts Romanian business organizations regardless of their majority shareholder, size, type, and location under the pressure of catching up and to assimilate the new "rules of the game" called the 21st-century market competition. Romanian business organizations must be innovative, creative and resourceful in their global quest for sustainable competitive advantage.

The Romanian business organization has embraced the challenges and opportunities of the information age indicated by most of the questionnaire respondents due to also requirements of their mother companies.

The presence and usage of IT&C technology are not enough if the provided data, information, and knowledge are not capitalized and leverage to its maximal extent. 2018 Romania is facing both ends of the IT&C adoption, high tech, and globally competitive business organizations that have emerged and business organizations that are still run with very rudimentary and basic IT&C support.

Over the years Romania has become an IT&C knowledge pool that is worldwide recognized and appreciated mainly not by local Romanian business organizations but more by foreign, local operating, business organizations.

**Presently** the Romanian economy is not ready to change and to create value also from data, information and knowledge that it owns. The first steps have been already made, Romania has one of the best internet infrastructures in the world, placing the country permanently in the top 5 worldwide.

There is still a considerable share of business organizations that have are not ready to change and to jump into the new data, information and knowledge-driven economy. At the level of top management and driven by the foreign majority shareholders local business organizations have adopted and implemented the concepts of value management and value recognition within their business processes.

There are companies that realized the hidden potential of value management and value assessment and usage and have set up value-driven business processes. The knowledge created by business organizations is stored and disseminated within their organizations.

The acknowledgment of value contribution from business support activities is still in the early stages. Many of the business support services are still tributary to the industrial, classical perception as value consumers and not as value creators and drivers.

The capitalization of knowledge and information from business support services is still in its early stages, many of the expressed opinions indicated the need for more change in this aspect to assure the needed innovation and sustainable competitive advantage that Romanian business organizations need for the global competition.

The "late start" in the information age change process can be considered an opportunity that the Romanian business environment must make the most of to be able to increase its competitiveness. Most of the respondents indicated that value, value management, and value-based management is an opportunity that must be capitalized.

Business support services are still in the early stages of the change process towards being a decisive and certain business value creator.

Accounting (financial and management accounting) are still not used to their maximal potential for the business decision process and for business management. Romanian financial statutory accounting is still very much tax-driven and nowhere close to provide business management and business process relevant information.

Management accounting is still not completely capitalized especially through the perspective of the information age where the new technological IT&C breakthroughs have made better data processing and dissemination possible.

Romanian accounting is still very reactive (not proactive), not very much IT&C support driven, and not business proactive through the usage of available data, information, and knowledge that resides in business support activities.

Legal services have not a considerable business impact on the business value creation process due to the lack of communication. Most legal services are still used only to "secure and mitigate" business risks and transactions, no considerable or material involvement in M&A transactions is present.

Human Resources Management is having one of the highest perception scores in the value creator role and create value due to the proximity to the operational part of the business activities.

IT&C is present and defines itself as a solid and definitive hurdle in the 21$^{st}$-century globalized business environment by enabling and leveraging the needed and owned data, information and knowledge. IT&C has become the tool for managing and running the 21$^{st}$-century information age determined markets and business organizations.

Procurement is still in its early stage, not many business organizations have capitalized and gained competitive advantages through it. The essence of a profitable, efficient and performant procurement lies within accurate, timely and accessible information that has been enabled by the information age.

Only about 50% of the respondents have embraced and use value-driven performance evaluation tools and concepts. This indicates still a high resilience to the challenges and opportunities of the information age.

By recognition, acknowledgment, and valuation of the available untapped information pool, further improvements and efficiency increments can be achieved. Most of the respondents have also indicated the clear need to develop themselves, to adapt and adopt the realities of the "new economy" where data, information and knowledge are the "prime commodity".

The knowledge pool from within the business organizations residing in the business support activities is mainly unused due to lack of information, willingness, knowledge, and economic reason. Most of the business support activities need to start their morphing from the "classical" approach to the knowledge and business value driver.

Further, you'll find the specific conclusions for the researched business support activities. The specific conclusions are based on factual evidence of the questionnaire and on conceptual deep research. The conclusions represent an as-is status and give some hints and recommendations regarding the next steps.

## 4.1 Conclusions - Value management

The concepts of value, value management and the corresponding valuation and measurement methods and principles have been at the center of human attention from very early times.

The theory of value has always been a mirror of the concerns of human society. At the same time and at the same rate the concept of value and value management have also developed the accompanying concepts of value evaluation and measurement have evolved and developed. The increase in complexity and reach also determined an increase in accuracy and difficulty of the value measuring and evaluation methods and principles.

The value concept will have to change and adjust to today's new economy, an economy based on data, information and knowledge. The change of the value concept needs to reflect the new *hard facts* of the new economy, the change needs to somehow reflect the subjective and objective value of information and knowledge.

Value creation for its shareholders is the ultimate goal of any business organization. The generic economic process and the business processes have value embedded in their core and can be considered as the main driver for development and evolution.

Value as a concept and the thereof depending on economic and business processes have evolved and transformed over time due to the change and evolution of the human society and the determining driving factors and forces towards evolution.

The business organization has traditionally focused on the fine-tuning and optimization of the direct value flows that handle the tangible aspects of the business activity. The development of the tangible aspects has followed and is in sync with the development of the economic model an asymptotic path.

Alongside the development of the economic models, the complexity has also followed the same path.

To be more innovative and to meet the contemporary business requirements all business organizations must innovate and become more creative until the next breakthrough in science that will enable the next major extensive wave of development. The innovation requirements force business organizations to look at their internal untapped growth potentials that are in their intangible assets that gain increased momentum and become critical for any business.

The business support services, the indirect business activities, have been *left behind* the development and optimization of the direct business activities.

From the today's perspective value and value management, if handled properly, are *escaping* the classical view of cost-cutting and are transforming into prized business support tools and services that can influence any business organization result.

M. Porter's classical value chain model has also illustrated the collaboration, layout, and interaction of direct and indirect business activities to attain the value-creating competitive advantage. The complexity of value creation and determination for business organizations comes out of the changing of the role and importance of the business activities. If we consider the vertical activities of Porter's value chain model the direct activities, then we have indirect activities laid out transversal through the business organization.

The economic and social development converges towards intangibles, data and information are becoming the main driver of everything else. In the future, the role of the indirect business activities will increase and gain momentum, while the pace of the extensively developed direct activities will decrease.

Research opportunities will arise from the change in momentum of the business direct and indirect activities that will be supported and transformed also be future technological advances in information technology.

The role and importance of the business transversal, today support, indirect activities will determine a change process also at the macro and micro level of the global and local economies.

Despite all the changes in business activities, regardless of tangible or intangible asset driven, must comply and conform to the goal of a business organization of creating value and wealth for shareholders.

## 4.2  Conclusions - Knowledge, Knowledge-based economy and organizations

The information age and the knowledge economies have triggered irreversible changes in the world, the business organization had to adapt and adopt the new lifestyle and values.

The presence of a new type of worker, the knowledge worker, needed from the existing concepts an urgent and deep transformation to be able to cope with the requirements of the *new knowledge-driven economy and society.*

The era of information is here to stay, the changes determined by the development and evolution of information technology have left serious and permanent changes in human social development and in most sciences. The rapid evolution of high-tech information software and hardware enabled a development loop that has no foreseeable and imaginable result.

Knowledge lives on data and information that is and will be increasingly accessible and available. Knowledge has its root in trial and error evolutionary steps that resulted from the lessons learned of past events.

Knowledge management and all related aspects like knowledge-based economy, knowledge-based organizations and their knowledge workers are concepts still in their early stages. The science of knowledge took off only in the last two decades and has still a long way to develop.

Science and knowledge management will be massively supported also be the new technologies like artificial intelligence, real-time big data, machine learning, etc. Opportunities will arise from the new challenges of technological developments that drive the transformation of human society and its depending systems.

Knowledge is the capital of today and will be the capital of tomorrow's reality. By fostering and growing the knowledge capital alongside the transformation of classical economical processes, concepts and models the sustainability and ability to compete in new economic environments can be assured by the business organizations of the 21st century.

Research opportunities will arise alongside the development of technology that will enable the transformation of tacit knowledge into explicit knowledge and their distribution to all sides involved.

In today's business organizations, the indirect activities, the intangible assets of the business must be involved and must contribute with their fair share of value and knowledge towards the result of the business operations. The indirect activities, the business support activities must have the support of science and technology to rise from their undercapitalized and underestimated role in the context of a knowledge economy and knowledge-based organizations. The biggest research challenge will be the determination, safekeeping, and valuation of the tacit knowledge from within organizations. Tacit knowledge is gaining more importance and reputation as a solid contributor to the result of a business.

The competitive advantage in today's knowledge-based economy is ensured through science, innovation, qualified workforce and the wide usage of knowledge.

The knowledge of today will transform and create the reality of tomorrow.

## 4.3   Conclusions - Financial accounting

The shareholder value creation process has become a process that is needed and demanded by all stakeholders of a business organization like shareholders, investors, executives, and managers and other 3rd party stakeholders.

Business organizations must overcome one major obstacle of the *new economy* to be able to be a sustainable, flourishing organization. Today's business organization must deliver excellence in their activity by creating a constant and predictable shareholder value flow.

Innovation and creativity must become the focus of business organizations to be able to create value. A detailed, exhaustive analysis is needed at all levels of business processes to ensure that any growth and value potentials are accessed and used.

Growth and profitability during the industrial revolution have been made by focusing on the extensive development of direct productive business activities.

The increase in competition complexity determined by the triggered challenges of the information age and the complexity of internationalization and globalization has led the business organization to look to unexploited value flow generators and growth potentials within their own organizations, the business support activities.

The value stream of a business organization is built on value streams that come from direct and from indirect business activities.

The 21st-century accounting activity is built on two major areas, financial accounting and management accounting that have transformed the business organization and the way of doing business by embracing the challenges of the *new economy*. The *classical* role of accounting as a *bean counter* and *record keeper* has been shed and considered obsolete. In the *new economy* accounting, financial and management accounting is providing proactive data, information and knowledge that will enable a better and much more accurate business management decision process.

The 21st-century accounting, financial accounting and management accounting, has become one of the major adopters and users of IT&C technology and developed to be a solid and sustainable business data and information supplier for the business organization's management decision process. Especially management accounting is driving and demanding more complex and accurate IT tools for today's modern business intelligence.

The characteristic of business value is that it is business-specific and subjective especially for intangible, immaterial business services and activities. One tool derived from residual income, economic value added (EVA), can be used to highlight the contribution to the shareholder value creation process by business support activities.

The deliverable of accounting is a textbook intangible asset of a business organization that makes use of the high-end IT technology to enable relevant and in time business information.

Financial accounting is without a doubt a complex and not extremely easy to understand and to follow business activity being driven and imposed by the government through their financial and fiscal policy. The policies imposed by fiscal state authorities are not always business value creation oriented, states through their fiscal authorities need to assure financing for state expenditure that do not always affect or sustain business organizations, like social protection, defense, financing of state-owned public companies, etc.

Therefore, the understanding and application of fiscal regulations demand skilled and trained professional that understand the purpose and scope of all regulations imposed. These skilled professionals translate the fiscal requirements that impact the business organization's operations by the creation and sending of knowledge to all involved business sub-organizations.

The developments in IT have made it possible that most accounting bookings are done automatically without the earlier clerical activity. The focus in financial accounting has shifted towards the cost reduction of accounting transactions by the adoption of IT tools and systems that make accounting a *standardized* activity that enables the statutory conformance to fiscal rules and regulations. This alignment to the fiscal rules and regulations implies fiscal and financial accounting knowledge translated into speedy and reliable IT systems to automate most of the transactions.

The booked transactions create value to the business organization by having reliable and accurate bookings about past business transactions. The post-fact analysis of past business transactions supports the business organization's future planning and management of business transactions.

Further, the financial accounting alignment of business organizations to statutory rules and regulations enables the safe business operation and compliance to certain markets governed by different national states.

Financial accounting is creating, distributing, and using knowledge in its financial statements and financial statutory reports that enable the safe and predictable business operation on any world market by alignment to the statutory rules and regulations.

The adoption of modern IT system tools and systems gives a differentiator to business organizations by cost reduction, increased public transparency and statutory compliance and speedy and accurate up to date financial records.

The usage of automated IT tools, like artificial intelligence, that recognize patterns and rules for financial accounting can add and create even more knowledge and value to operating business organizations. The usage of automated tools can enable more rapid and easy access to financial and international markets by the adoption of automated application and adoption of IFRS (International Financial Reporting Standards) that facilitates also for investors an easier way of comparing their investment opportunities.

Today's financial accounting has just started the adoption of automated modern IT tools and systems that transform the way financial statutory accounting has been done.

Because of the external stakeholder view of financial accounting the value creation process. The external stakeholder, governments through their financial and fiscal authorities can distort the value creation process for the business organization up to its cancellation.

In the case of financial accounting, the knowledge creation process is unchanged by the external stakeholder, the political and social orientation of the market regulator can massively alter the business value creation process.

Financial accounting is a knowledge-based organization that is delivering business value to its external stakeholders based on the political and social orientation of the market regulator.

## 4.4    Conclusions - Management accounting

Considering the *new economy,* an economy driven by data and information, we can see management accounting being transformed and driven towards the massive enablement of more and complex data analysis, past and future related. The non-productive, value consuming view of the business support activities have been made obsolete.

Management accounting has come a long way from simplistic cost calculation to business value driver by the best and efficient usage of existing business resources and adoption of the challenges of the information age.

The 21st-century management accounting has proven itself as a solid and sustainable, data and information-driven business value driver that is contributing and supporting the business management and steering process. A constitutive part of the business model of the *new economy* will include de strategic management accounting that is supporting the planning and management of past, present and future business.

Management accounting as a knowledge-based organization is contributing to the business value creation process of the business organization that is pursuing a sustainable competitive advantage that enables the adaptation and adjustment to the demanding and challenging business environment of the *new economy*.

Management accounting is, compared to financial accounting, a relatively young discipline that came to respond to the need of business organization management to understand what is going on in their business.

If financial accounting is focused on the financial statements and external 3rd parties than management accounting is focused on business management information that is used internally in the business organization.

Financial accounting is governed by external parties, financial and fiscal authorities and reflects the interest of those authorities as governing organizations of the respective market. Management accounting is focused on understanding what is happening in the business organization and what can be done from the business organization perspective to mitigate variances from the strategic business goal.

The key differentiating factor of financial accounting and management accounting is the different stakeholder view; financial accounting is addressing the external stakeholder whereas management accounting is focusing on the internal business organization stakeholder.

The different view of the addressed business stakeholder is also defining the way and type of created, used, and transmitted knowledge and value. Management accounting is using and distributing business organization internal knowledge based on the current operations and on data recorded and provided by financial accounting. Management accounting professionals are skilled and trained professionals that must have a multidisciplinary view on business operations results that need to be aligned with the business organization's goals.

The output of management accounting is delivering reliable and sustainable data and information for the management decision process. Relying on past financial data, recorded by financial accounting, management accounting is looking to the future and aligning with business organization's goals is delivering the needed management decision data and information.

Management accounting is the typical knowledge-based organization; it uses its knowledge to process and transform the created financial accounting knowledge for the creation and distribution of business operations data and information.

The output of management accounting is business case-specific, it can be supported and enhanced by the usage of modern and complex business IT systems like big data, business intelligence, business workflows automation, data visualization tools, etc.

Management accounting professionals rely on their tacit knowledge to build, transform, and distribute business case-specific data and information that can not only support the management decision process but can also drastically change its result.

The value creation process is highly business-specific and is enhanced by modern business management that is based on data and information rather than on an autocratic business management view. The value creation process is assured by specific business case data and information that meet the needs of business management responsibilities.

Modern management accounting is a deeply business operational involved management tool that accompanies and drives the business operations by having broad access and understanding of all business-relevant data and information from external and internal sources.

The consolidation and usage of all business-relevant data and information, the created business-specific knowledge can be capitalized and turned into business competitive differentiating value.

The value creation process can be distorted and transformed into the value consumption process if the provided data and information are not adopted adequately by all levels of the business organization.

Today's information age modern business organization cannot afford to be managed like in the industrial age, where operational excellence was the focus.

The today's business organizations can compete on a globalized, speedy, and complex environment only by adhering and aligning to the business value creation process; operational excellence is the yesterday's competitive advantage and the today's norm.

The differentiation factor in the modern business organization is the value created by internal indirect productive activities, like management accounting that by having a broad business view can steer and drive the knowledge and value creation of the business organization.

The successful change process towards the adoption and usage of the available business data and information is the main sustainable competitive advantage factor that needs to be used and adopted by all levels of the business organization.

Management accounting is a management tool that needs to be assimilated to today's 21st-century business organizations regardless of their object of activity without external or internal non-business-related influencing factors.

## 4.5    Conclusions - Legal services

The legal function is part of the business support services that are also recognized as secondary activities by the Value Chain concept of Porter. Together with other business support services, legal services, build the foundation of firm infrastructure that assures the general business framework.

Legal services, especially corporate business legal services are a safeguarding measure of society that handles potential business risks by regulating and formalizing business transactions and defining market rules and regulations. Like the position of financial and management accounting, legal services can mitigate and regulate potential risks and business transactions for business organizations based on existing legal frameworks. Law professionals, lawyers, are trained, skilled professionals that give assurance for business organizations by designing and adapting legal documents to assure and safeguard specific business transactions or business relations.

Based on their role, corporate lawyers, "defend" their business organization by creation and adjustment of contracts, agreements, frameworks, etc. that enables the involved parties to have a decent and risk-free business transaction or business relationship.

The specific legal business knowledge creation is the key and defining factor of corporate business law, the distribution to internal and external stakeholders of the created knowledge is the enabling factor of the created corporate legal knowledge. Corporate legal services rely also on precedents of similar business cases, therefore meeting also the data and information storage and processing element of the knowledge-based organization.

Corporate legal services are a mandatory activity in the 21st-century modern business organization that is influenced by the increase in complexity of business transactions determined by globalization, changes in socio-political environments and information and data abundance. The created business knowledge is impartial to the information age; it is enabled and potentiated by the discoveries and developments of information technology by assuring more easy access to a relevant business existing knowledge and by enabling a higher degree in transparency.

The value creation process of business legal services is specific and relies on external factors, the successful closing of the specific business transaction and internal factors like the tacit internal legal knowledge of the law professional.

The value creation process of the business legal services can be disrupted by external factors like socio-political changes and orientation of the business framework. More liberal, democratic countries tend to have more business value created by their corporate legal services while countries that are more conservative and autocratic have the business value creation diminished and more oriented towards risk mitigation.

Because of the complexity and specialization of business transactions, legal services are often outsourced and used based on the specific needed legal business knowledge. The value creation process is potentiated, enabled, and assured by the specificity of legal requirements and by the permissiveness of general socio-political frameworks.

## 4.6    Conclusions - Human Resources

HRM has increasingly increased in complexity because of the changing market requirements and competition. The created value and the resulting competitive advantage have put business organizations into the position to assure and to sustain the growing reach of HRM in the business value chain.

Human resources are one of the most important and relevant business functions and activities that need to be treated with the utmost attention by business managers, stakeholders, and shareholders. Based on the existing business goals the activity of the human resource must find, acquire, retain and develop the needed business human resources by aligning and understanding the business strategic goals.

By assuring the needed employees, human resources (HR) defines, develops, and distributes specific activity and business knowledge. The knowledge creation and management process are influenced by HR in two ways, by creation, implementation, and management of rules and regulations for internal business use and by sourcing of employees that contribute to the overall business knowledge creation and management.

The creation and management of internal rules and regulations for employed staff are based on existing legal frameworks, the tacit knowledge of HR staff and business organization goals and organizational culture.

Knowledge is created by adjusting the HR rules for the achievement of business goals. In the case of HR knowledge creation is the basis of the organizational culture that transforms and adjusts the "level" of the business organization so that tacit knowledge is transformed in explicit knowledge by its employees and fosters the learning organization.

Business value is created by the sourced, retained, and developed staff that assures and enables further development of business organization and operations. In the information age, the information worker, the knowledge worker, is enabling, transforming, and distributing knowledge and create business value true the shaped, improved and streamlined operational and organizational business processes, tools and systems.

The main challenge for the HR of the 21st information is the sourcing, retention, and development of needed skilled and trained human resources that can contribute to the knowledge and value creation process of the business organization.

The HR function has transcended the clerical, administrative role and has morphed into a creative, proactive knowledge-based organization that is contributing to the business organization value creation process by tapping into the core of the knowledge creation and development, the tacit knowledge transformation from tacit into explicit knowledge by creating an adequate framework for the employed staff.

Disruptions in the knowledge and value creation process can be determined by socio-political instability, increased labor union power, missing or low management performance and lack of clear business goals and perspectives that determine a decrease in employee and employer branding.

Human resources in the information age is a delicate balance between demand and supply of needed skilled resources that can be acquired by business organizations that are proactively and flexibly acting on the labor market.

## 4.7 Conclusions Information technology

To profit from all IT benefits the management of a business organization must be ready to adopt change and update and adapt to the latest market requirements.

IT has evolved a developed from being an aid for certain calculus tools to a real and consistent ecosystem of tools and systems that have decisive business support and driver functions. The 21st-century business organizations must face a huge amount of daily new data and information that might impact or influence their business. To manage all the data and information and turn it into useful business intelligence business organizations must adopt and promote adequate software and hardware solutions that allow them to acquire, process, store and communicate relevant business data and information.

To be able to adapt, act and react to the ever-changing market requirements, business organizations must focus on the actual business support functions, information technology is one of the support / indirect business functions, and reconsider their classical role as business support services.

Information technology is enabling the untapped resources that business organizations have in their already owned data and information. Software is heavily supported by modern and powerful hardware that empowers business organizations to use data and information insights by using modern technologies like big data, data cubes, analytical data processing, artificial intelligence, machine learning, etc.

The increased accessibility of modern technology, especially information technology allows business organizations to make the most of available data and information that previously remained untapped.

The near future will bring again new developments and breakthroughs that will rewrite classical concepts and will allow companies to capitalize on the new possibilities. IT is no longer a resource-consuming business function, it has transformed into a clear and decisive business driver and value creator. The future developments in IT will allow having even more reliable data and information that can be used by business organizations to gain the needed competitive advantage.

Information technology, used as a very broad term, is the driving force of the information age that has transformed and changed many aspects of human society. The key element of the information age is data and information that are processed and distributed by highly complex and performant software and hardware systems.

The essence of information technology (IT) is the management of huge and complex volumes of data that are generated by human activity. The information age has taken the discoveries and developments of the industrial revolution and put them through the next progress step of the information age.

IT has enabled business organizations to become more dynamic and more accurate in their decision processes that led to better and more sustainable business developments. The IT function of a business organization became an integral and decisive factor of competitive and sustainable companies. The more the adoption of IT modern technologies is assured the more competitive differentiation arguments a business organization has.

IT is at the pinnacle of data and information management of the 21st century that is based on already *commoditized* services like basic network infrastructure and services and on business-specific software and hardware systems. The knowledge creation, processing, storage, and dissemination process is digital, it feeds all needed internal stakeholders and should self-adjust to the requirements of the new digital informational markets. Corporate IT quickly became the differentiating factor of the information age. The modern technology has enabled and redefined the means of knowledge management from creation to dissemination.

The IT tools used today are evolving and are re-defining once again the classical concepts driven by the need for better alignment of used systems and tools to the requirements of a dynamic changing market environment.

IT has allowed fast access and accurate business data processing that can be used for automation and improved and efficient business processes. The value proposition of information technology is incontestable; the provided possibilities exceed everything that was considered *state of the art* in the industrial age. IT has led business organizations into the 21st century and away from analogic, mechanical, limited means of the earlier age.

IT is contributing to the business organization value creation process by highly accurate, fast and complex systems that capitalize on the relevant business information that allows companies to differentiate themselves from other business organizations.

Information technology has enabled and made possible massive developments towards increased efficiency, accuracy, reliability and speed by innovations and inventions of technological means that completely transformed and made obsolete some of the classical concepts like analog communication, fax services, written communication, data acquisition and processing, etc.

The challenges of modern fast-moving business organizations for the coming years will be the creation and usage of IT tools and systems that allow relevant data query and filtering that enable pattern recognition and reliable future steps models to be created and used for future predictive business management decision process through automated and/or artificial intelligence.

## 4.8   Conclusions Procurement

From basic business, financial perspective one of the main benefits of procurement is cost savings through best available acquisitions of needed goods and services.

Procurement understands the business organization's needs and can act upon them through operational or tactical procurement and through strategic procurement.

The operational or tactical procurement enables, simply viewed, the business operations by assuring the right supplies at the right time for business operations. A lot of operational and tactical details are discussed and negotiated by procurement professionals that are involved in operational business activities.

The operational or tactical procurement activities can often be found in production business organizations as being part of supply chain management (SCM). SCM has operational and tactical responsibilities for business operations and implies operational knowledge and value management. Operational or tactical procurement implies a deep understanding of business operations, needing specific knowledge being used and created as well as value creation through business operations.

The strategic procurement or strategic sourcing has a broader view of business operations and has a focus on margin achievement as a business strategic goal.

The broader- and long-term view of procurement implies a thorough, deep, and multidisciplinary understanding of business processes.

The successful strategic procurement implies procurement professionals that make use of their knowledge to create procurement knowledge for the business organization that can be used and adjusted for the operational sub-organizations.

The usage of the created strategic procurement framework, the created procurement knowledge, is considered successful if it is supporting and driving the achievement of a business strategic goal, value creation for its shareholders.

The created specific knowledge, of procurement operational, tactical, and strategic, is creating value and driving the business by the short and long-term view of its core activity supplying needed goods and services as a driver for future operations.

Furthermore, the long-term view of strategic procurement is enabling and fostering the alignment of the procurement goals with the business goals. The resulting value and value creation are ongoing and are part of the continuous improvement process of the modern 21st-century modern business organization.

The procurement activity has simple financially quantifiable contributions, procurement savings and its implications, and value-creating factors driven by the long-term view of the strategic sourcing process.

Procurement has become a critical and vital business activity that relies, especially in the information age, on the knowledge of skilled and trained professionals that assure and drive the business value creation process through proper and adequate procurement of goods and services through the main procurement processes operational, tactical, and strategic procurement.

Procurement has evolved from the classical clerical nonproductive business activity to the strategic business partner function that creates and promotes the value and knowledge creation process.

The information age has transformed the classical procurements concepts, it enabled business organizations to make a huge qualitative jump by introducing all benefits of digital data processing and data communication.

Corporate business procurement has been empowered to operate globally by matching and tapping into all business supply requirements. At the same time, corporate procurement has made a big step towards alignment with the business organization's goals.

By understanding and aligning to the strategic business goals procurement has created specific matching supply policies and alternatives. The strategic alignment of business procurement gave companies the possibility to streamline their financial and supply position and to assure one of the main business inputs, the supply.

Knowledge creation is assured by streamlining the supply process and assimilation of change by the usage of modern information-driven tools and systems. Value creation is based mainly on the savings potential of the procurement activity but also on the long-term strategic view of corporate procurement programs that integrate also down-and up-stream supply activities.

The digital procurement, also known as e-procurement, has made an accurate and fast process possible that assured the needed competitive advantages for the business organization before they became affected by the information age obsolesce of data and information.

By adherence to the information age principles and ways, procurement became a wide-reaching and accurate business activity that can create knowledge and value for the business organization through fast, efficient and reliable supply sources.

## 4.9   Conclusions Value chain

Business support services are considered indirect productive business activities that do not add value to the business value chain.

For a long time, the business support services have been considered value consuming clerical activities that do not drive the business. Michael Porter has shown, through his value chain concept, that the business support activities have a clear and decisive contribution to the achievement of the business margin.

Per Porter's value chain concept, business support activities are nominated as secondary activities that support all business operational activities, the primary activities. Porter has published his value chain concept in 1985 at the dawn of the information age.

After more than 30 years from making the value chain concept public, the principles of the value chain remain unchanged, business activities contribute to the achievement of the business organization's goal, the business margin.

In the last 30 years, the information age has made many classical concepts outdated and others suffered drastic changes. The information age has determined huge changes in mindset, way of thinking and classical organizational operational steps.

The main *commodity* of the information age is data and information and its higher-level consolidation stages like knowledge and wisdom.

Since the early stage of human development, the key and most basic driver of human development was the quest and competition for data and information about distinct aspects of life like resources, understanding of the surroundings, territory, space, nature, etc.

Based on the newly acquired data and information humans could evolve and develop into today's world. At the first stages of development, humans have focused on resources and assets that drove observations of their surroundings that they could capitalize on and use in their favor.

For example, the caveman has been mostly interested in where to find food, water, and shelter. Only later humans have created tools that made the foraging, hunting, and shelter better. The acquired data and information have been passed along through generations. The incipient basic principles of the information age have been created, data, information was created and was passed on to the next generations starting with petroglyphs.

If we extrapolate human development from caveman to the 21st century it can be observed that the concepts of knowledge and value are the foundation of human development. Over time data and information is created, processed, improved, stored, and communicated through the own group or organization. The development and the higher-level consolidation of acquired data and information have led to the creation of new and development of previously acquired knowledge.

History has shown that value creation is of utmost importance for evolution and has proven to be a constant dominant concept. Over time valuable and useful concepts have prevailed while others have lost importance or became obsolete or irrelevant.

The information age has determined increased changes in all areas of human society. Today home use hardware and software are leaps away from the capabilities and potentials of the beginning of the information revolution.

The information has changed and transformed all aspects in the way business is done, it has rewritten the *rules of the game* especially in privately owned business organizations.

The information age has changed competition in three ways:

- The rules of the competition are altered and changed by affecting industry structures
- Competitive advantage is granted to the business organizations that embrace the requirements of the information age
- The challenges of the information age have generated new business ideas and new business organizations

The purpose and scope of privately-owned business organizations are still the same, the creation of sustainable value for its shareholders. The information revolution has changed aspects of the value chain and the value chain activities by linking and replacing more efficient and feasible IT related solutions to the classical approach.

When looking at the transformations that the business organizations have been going through in their pursuit of sustainable competitive advantage it shows the adaptations and adjustments that have been done in the primary and secondary business activities.

The information age is putting a major emphasis on data and information, it is shifting the attention from primary activities, that are commoditized, highly automated, and efficient.

The primary activities of the value chain are supported by secondary activities that have as their main output the creation, processing, and distribution of knowledge and value that support and drive the business organization.

The better the secondary activities, business support activities are working the more business value and knowledge are created. The more support is added from IT the more competitive differentiation, price reduction and competitive advantage are created.

The secondary value activities have gained a new role in the context of the information revolution. The business support activities have gained a clear and consistent new role in the information age business organization, the role of a business driver and a business creator.

The information revolution has made a big mark on human society, information technology has made huge jumps in terms of an increase in capacity and processing power since 1980 until now. It is also safe to assume that the next 30 years will bring at least the same amount of innovation and development until now.

Considering the above assumptions, how would the business support activities be like?

What would their role be, still secondary business support activities?

Could we call them as being primary business drivers?

Business support services have always been part of business organizations and have appeared and evolved as development and transformation of obsolete business processes to assure a more competitive, sustainable and efficient business process.

## 4.10 Conclusions Value-based performance metrics

Value-based management and knowledge management are some of the main concerns and challenges of the 21st century that is driven by the rapid development and adoption of information technology.

The financial accounting statutory based business performance evaluation has certain advantages and sure drawbacks. The value-based approach is trying to compensate for the shortcomings of the financial statutory accounting-based view by introducing the shareholder equity maximization concept as the main objective of the existence and operation of business organization and as a driver of the capital-driven economy.

Business performance will be an ever interesting and much-debated topic that will relate always to the value creation aspect. The value creation aspect highlighted by the presented value-driven indicators focuses on the shareholder equity maximization aspect thus on the shareholder value creation.

As per Porter's value chain concept, there are two activity types that contribute to the margin achievement of any business organization, primary and secondary or business support activities. The primary activities make widespread use of lean and kaizen concepts when approaching the value creation process.

Secondary activities have been deemed as being resources consuming and not having a clear and determinable contribution to the value creation process of the business organization.

By adopting value-based performance evaluation indicators, the value contribution is determinable and quantifiable and provides more detailed information for the management decision process.

The adoption of value-based management driven by the information age is an opportunity and an absolute must, for business organizations from all over the world, that want to compete in the changing world of the 21st century.

Most of the Romanian business organizations are still prone to the older industrial, strict organizational and management style that was defining and dominating the industrial age.

Through the adoption of value-based management Romanian business organizations have the opportunity to step up and evolve concerning the organizational and management style that drives further efficiency and profitability increments.

The *democratization* of data, information, and knowledge has changed the way business organizations are managed, operated and organized.

The high internet penetration degree and the above European average IT skills and literacy create the prerequisites to adopt the information age and the value-based management concepts and principles. Romanian business organizations must and have the potential and all prerequisites to assure themselves they need for sustainable competitive advantage in the globalized market competition.

The business support services in Romanian business organizations can also make the shift in paradigm to change from the *classical* view of resource-consuming to clear contributors to the business organization's value creation process.

The value concept is getting difficult to be observed when talking about the social involvement of companies through corporate social responsibilities (CSR) programs. Like any business-related activity also CSR is expected to have a return on the involved inputs.

Can the existing or presented concepts be used in the determination of the return of CSR programs, not really? CSR creates value for the business organization, it is an intangible value, as the value creation of the business support services, that still needs its adequate and correct measurement tools and concepts.

The transformations and changes in the information age are indubitable for human society. The value concept, as we know it today, will be pushed to its limits by the rise of artificial intelligence. Artificial Intelligence (AI) will be integrated into the daily life of humans and replace humans in certain activities.

More and more today considered *creative* human activities will be *operationalized* and much better executed by AI. Business organizations will adopt and use the new opportunities given by AI.

If the main purpose of a business organization is the shareholder value creation by equity maximization, how can the AI adoption transform this purpose? Where will be the created value? Who will benefit from the value?

Value-driven management is showing the performance of a business organization without having the drawbacks of the financial accounting statutory reporting and business performance evaluation system that is prone to manipulation. In a globalized more competitive economy, business support services will be transformed by the information age and will have data, information and knowledge at their core whereas the best usage of the existing knowledge and information will make the difference in business competition.

Companies compete for the best possible sustainable competitive advantage on an asymptotical, industrial age, development path where every contributing activity has to be leveraged, optimized and maximized.

## 4.11 Conclusions Economic value-added

The main idea behind EVA is that a business, regardless of accounting rules and regulations, is only then truly profitable when it creates value and wealth for its shareholders.

Value and wealth for shareholders go beyond the calculation of the accounting net income and profitability.

Economic value and shareholder wealth are created only if the business returns rate is above the cost of the employed capital.

The economic value concept summarizes how much value and from what business areas and components the value is created.

Through its defining elements, EVA succeeds to shift the focus only on income and revenue also to the balance sheet items of the respective business and is nurturing and promoting management decisions that also consider the assets part of the business not only the revenue and costs side.

The main most desired characteristic that the capital markets are looking in business is wealth and value creation and maximization for its shareholders.

EVA is the tool that is showing exactly the status of the investors' value and wealth generated or consumed by the invested in operation businesses. A clearer and more detailed EVA analysis are helping to go beyond the financial statements numbers and shows the value generators in the underlying business.

EVA is the mirror reflection of the company's real and true performance that also drives the desirability of the company's shares and prices per share on the capital markets.

The economic value-added concept is a relatively new and more complex concept that is able to measure value created for shareholders in a business organization.

The major change that is introduced by EVA is the consideration of the cost of capital. Any invested capital comes with its associated costs. To fulfill its scope and role, capital regardless of form, requires appropriate returns.

When evaluating business performance EVA is adjusting results with the cost of capital that is subject to investments and business risks that are leveraged and determined by uncertainty.

EVA comes as a quantifiable expression of value generated by any business organization.

Besides the *hard facts* of expressing the performance rendered by business organization EVA comes also with some fundamental requirements in business organizations like:

- A different view on management decisions not only at top management levels by considering the cost of capital.
- EVA requires a change in mindset at all levels of the organization towards the shareholder value creation view. EVA can be the basis of a modern quantifiable motivation system

Although the EVA concept has its challenges to be understood, handled, and implemented it has been shown that companies that use also EVA have had a real sustainable and solid development in the long run that increased the market value and business value. The major contribution to the development came from the change in the mindset of the organization, change that cannot be directly determined yet.

## 4.12 Conclusions Cash Value Added

The cash value-added model is focusing on value-creating activities while non-core activities are disregarded. The CVA (Cash Value Added) and CVA index model are straight forward methods to highlight the value creation aspect of the strategic business investments.

Strategic business investments are considered business projects and activities that assure and maintain the business operation and the business competitive advantage.

The CVA index drivers are elements that management can act upon and that provide clear and concise indicators of the wellbeing of the business operations.

CVA for a period is a good indicator of the business efficiency and profitability, it indicates if the business is self-sustaining and meeting the investors' expectations and requirements in terms of cash. The OCF – OCFD (OCF – operational cash flow; OCFD – operational cash flow demand) difference analysis can be done at any level of the business operations and can pinpoint the areas of business operations where additional attention is required.

Even though CVA is similar to Market Value Added, Stock measures and accounting profitability measures there are clear and distinct differences:

- Market value added is measured at a market level whereas CVA can be determined at the business unit level, project level, etc.
- Stock measures influence stocks at the present time while CVA can be

calculated at any time needed, past, present or future

- Accounting profitability like EBIT, EPS and Net income are disregarding the cost of capital whereas CVA is considering that a business must cover the operating and capital costs

## 4.13 Conclusions Economic Profit

Pushed by the shareholder's expectations and imposed by market regulators, state authorities' business organizations need to match and cope with all requirements of the 21st-century business environment.

Common and widely used performance measures have transformed and got "unhinged" from the core characteristics of doing business. Business organizations corporate governance and published results got disconnected form the core element of business, value and value creation.

Without disrupting already existing and functioning concepts and processes shareholders, stakeholders and management are looking and maintaining, besides the statutory reporting and perspective, management accounting reporting data. The latter is used for management decisions and management judgment of business performance that sustain the core ideas and strategic plans and perspectives of businesses.

Value-driven performance indicators consider the value aspect of the business activities by including the economic point of view when assessing business performance. The presented value-driven key performance indicators, EVA, CVA, and Economic Profit go further than classical financial accounting concepts and evaluate the value drivers of the respective business activities.

## 5 Final conclusions

The information age of the 21$^{st}$ century has determined irreversible and deep changes in the "classical" way of doing business. Slowly the "industrial age" style of managing a business is getting more and more obsolete due to the fundamental changes triggered by the "new economy" that is driven by data, information, and knowledge.

IT&C is omnipresent in the business organizations of the 21$^{st}$ century, regardless of type, size or company culture and values. Also, there is a certain irrefutable acceptance of the IT&C phenomenon, that has touched all business aspects and that is transforming and leading many "classic" concepts to the brink of obsolescence.

Leveraged by the information age value management is the "normal" response to the triggered changes. Even though the acceptance and recognition of the importance of value management are high (about 70%)

there are still 30% that are skeptical and that is not very convinced by the "new economy".

Most of the respondents indicated that the strategic orientation of their company is supporting the business value creation process through equity value maximization. Corporations have the lowest perception and acceptance, only 70%, when considering the vision, mission and values as a support of the value creation process through shareholder value maximization. This can partly be explained by the greatest "distance" from the shareholder in corporations whereas in small and mid-sized companies the proximity to the shareholder is an influencing factor.

When talking about knowledge and knowledge management corporations are scoring the lowest score at the perception and acceptance of knowledge and knowledge management. Generally, corporations tend to have a quite strict and comprehensive set of rules and procedures on what employees are expected to do and that covers mainly the operational aspects of the activity. Knowledge management and knowledge are mainly a high-level topic that is supposed to be on the activity list of the modern business manager and executive.

Business support activities, one of the most information, data, and knowledge-intensive business activities are perceived as being a value contributor to the business organization process with more than 95% of the opinions. The value creation of business support activities is considered as monitored only by 65% that is a considerable drop from the acknowledgment of the value contribution, from 95% to 65%. More than 35% do not consider or do not monitor the created value of indirect productive activities due to no involvement in the financial result of the business organization.

In their quest for the decisive sustainable competitive advantage companies of the 21st century must reinvent themselves and make maximum use of the data, information, and knowledge available within their own organizations.

The Romanian business environment is ready for the switch to the "new economy". There is the decisive need for a professional approach to value management, a value-driven management philosophy that does not leverage execution excellence and purely cash in the form of dividends but business value creation. Business value creation implies a change in management philosophy and repositioning in business operations towards the creation of economic value.

Tools like EVA©, CVA, and economic profit need to be internalized and used when evaluating business performance at M&A level or shareholder value creation level. The "industrial age" management perspective has to be changed for the economic value creation perspective. Economic value creation is a complex and wide-ranging concept that can transform and create a sustainable competitive advantage for any business organization irrespective of activity type, size and industry.

TopCFO is promoting and supporting the transformation towards the economic value creation of the 21st century "new economy".

For more details about the transformation process and support please contact TopCFO, www.TopCFO.ro

Item 1

Item 2

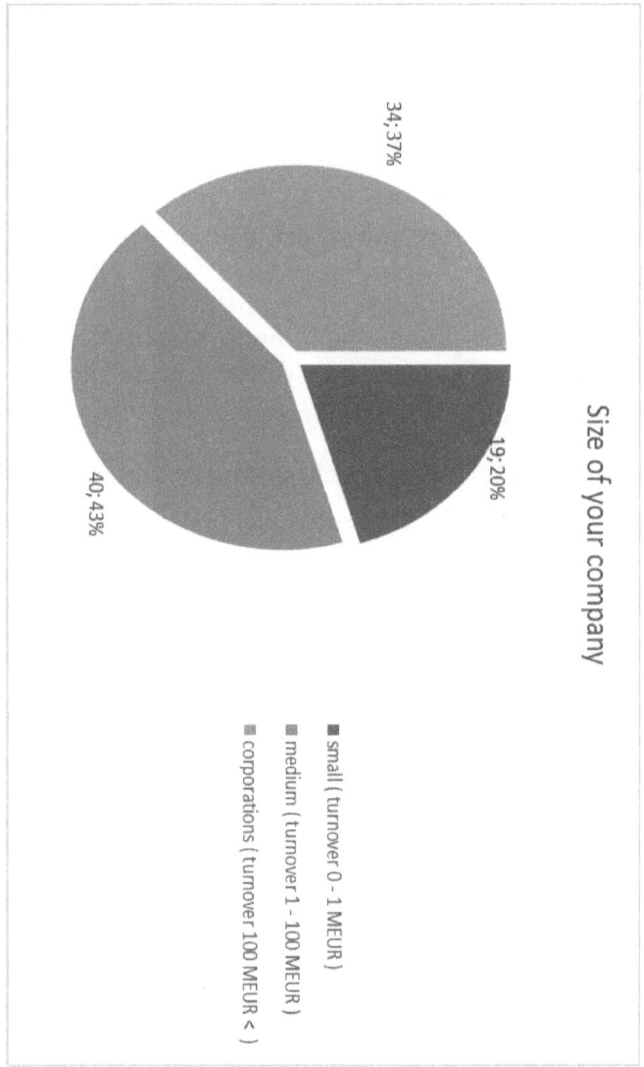

Item 3

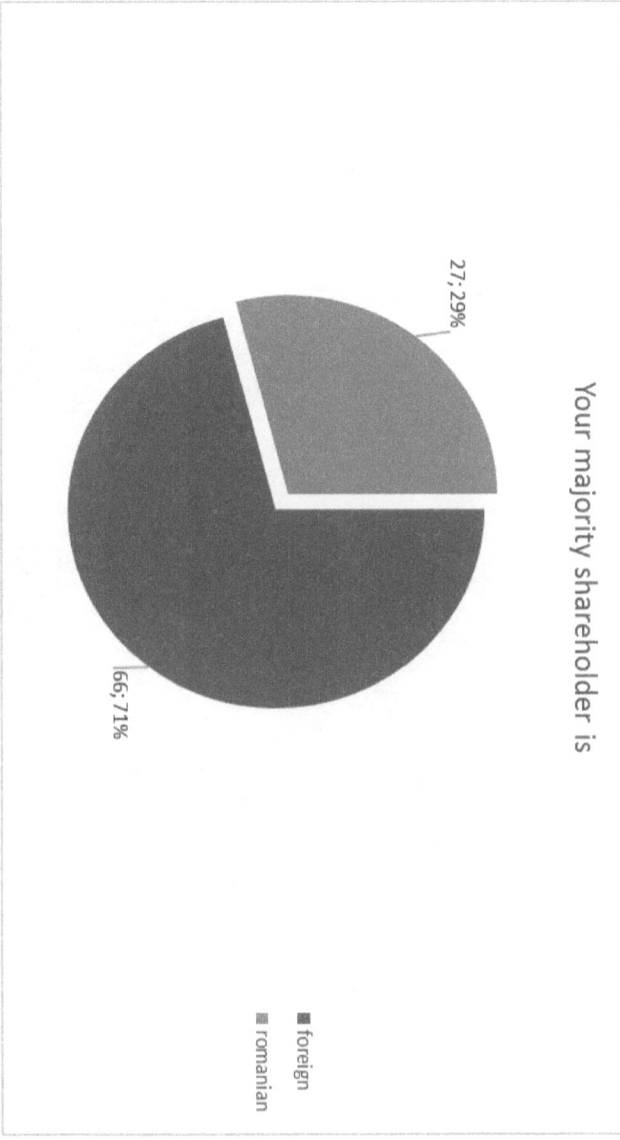

Your majority shareholder is

27; 29%

66; 71%

- foreign
- romanian

Item 4

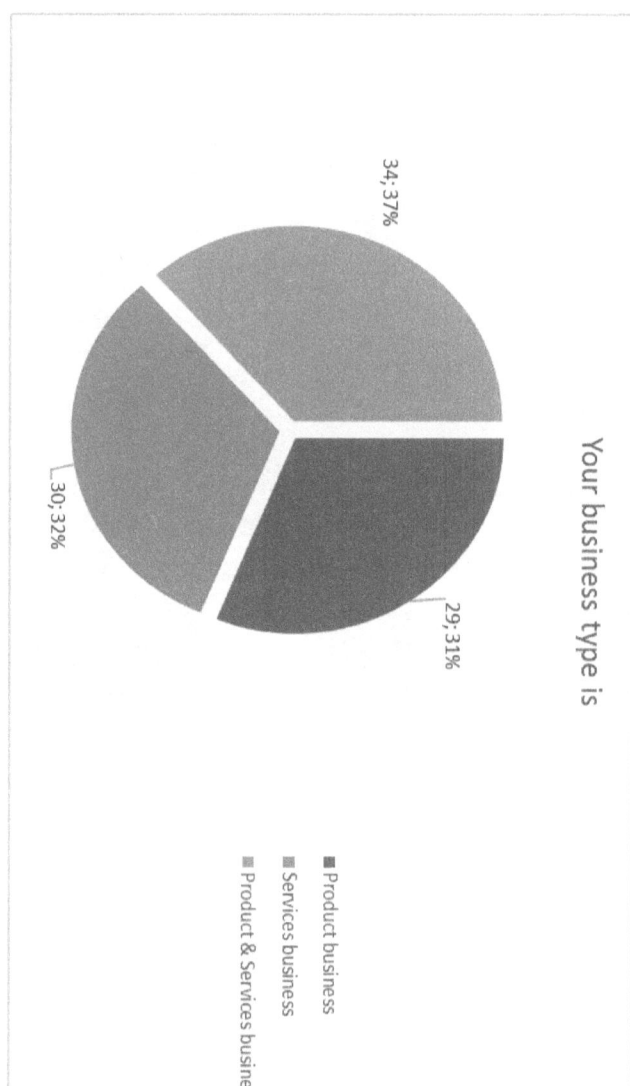

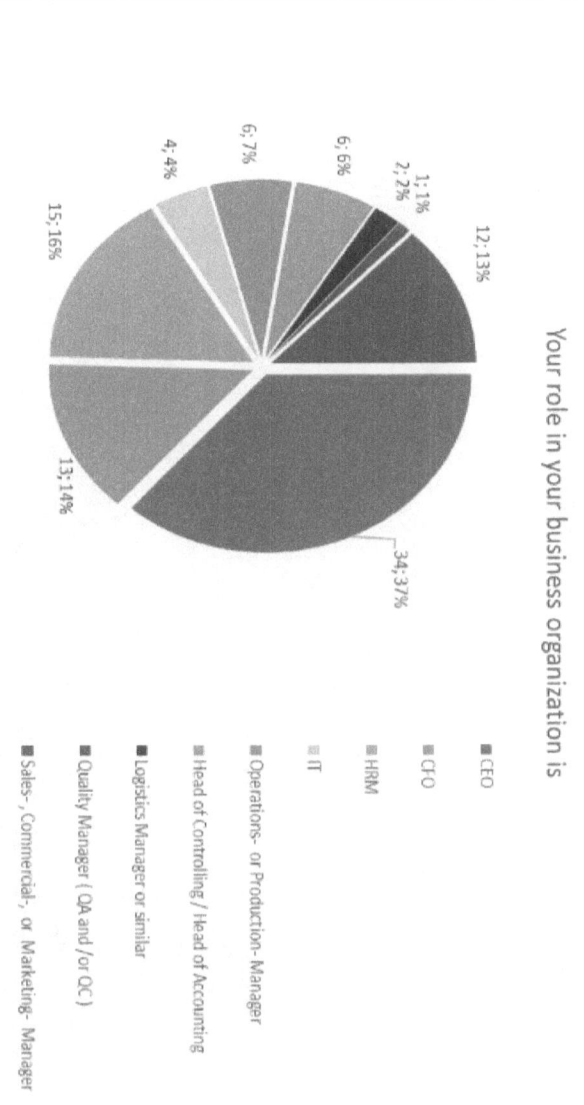

Your role in your business organization is

- CEO
- CFO
- HRM
- IT
- Operations- or Production- Manager
- Head of Controlling / Head of Accounting
- Logistics Manager or similar
- Quality Manager ( QA and /or QC )
- Sales- , Commercial-, or Marketing- Manager

Item 5

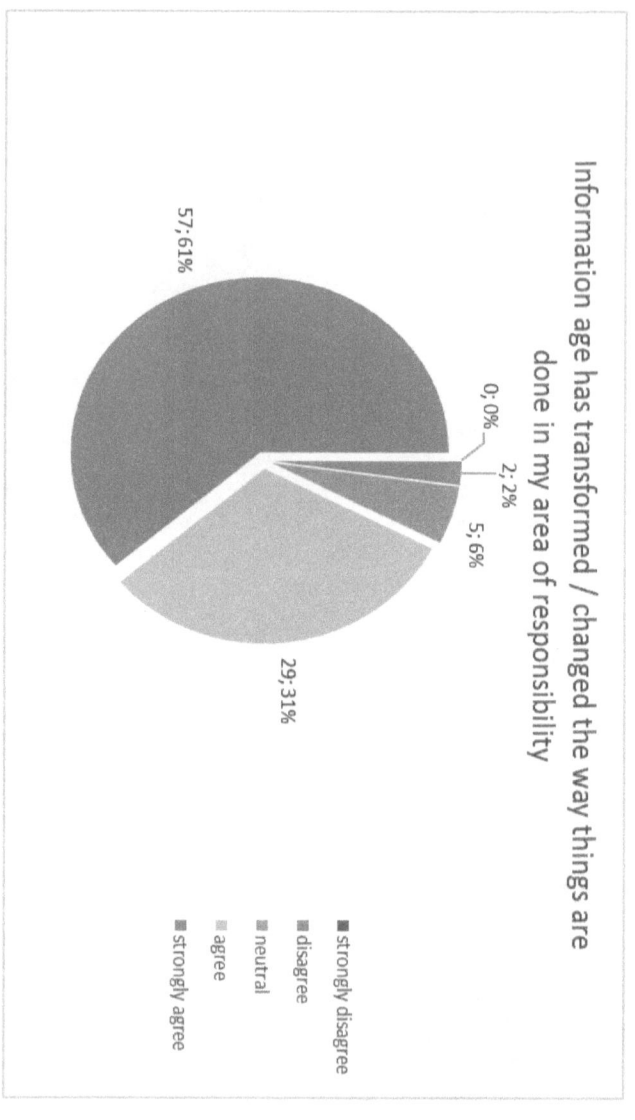

Item 6

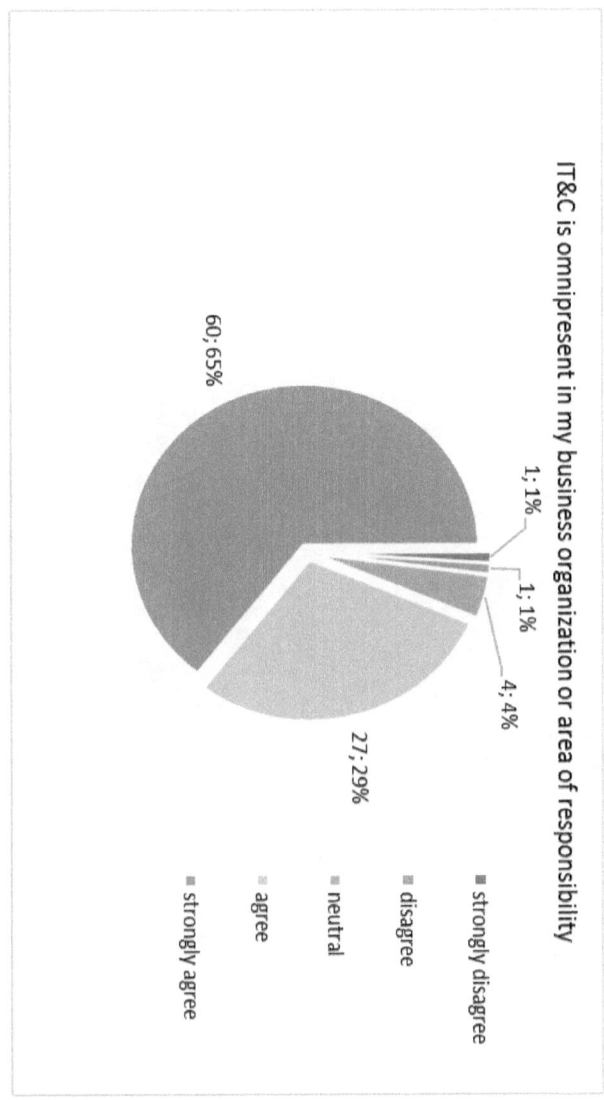

IT&C is omnipresent in my business organization or area of responsibility

- strongly disagree
- disagree
- neutral
- agree
- strongly agree

1; 1%
1; 1%
4; 4%
27; 29%
60; 65%

Item 7

Item 8

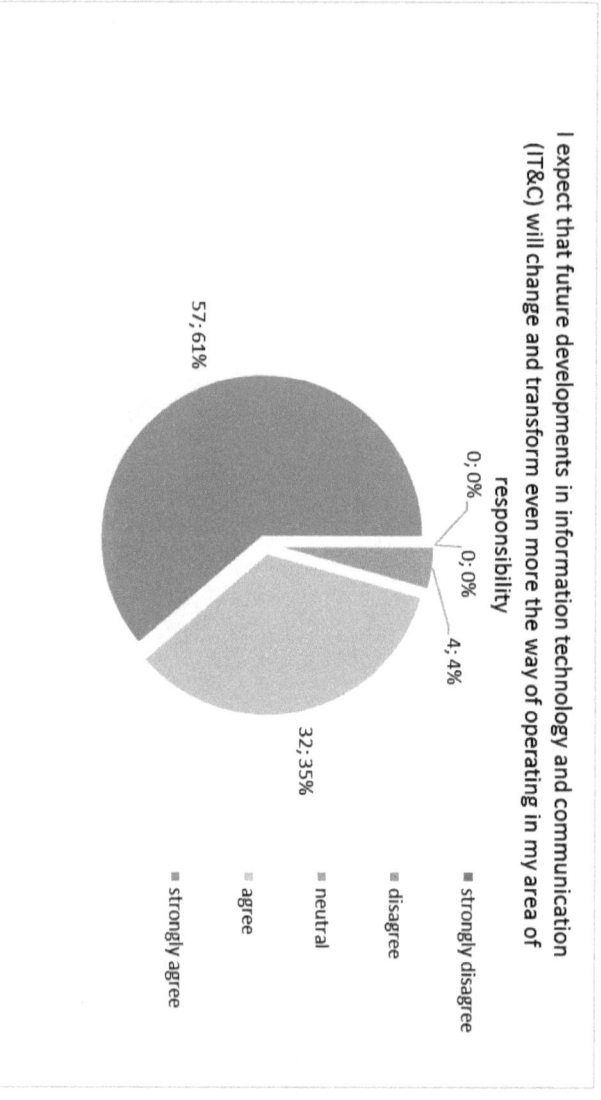

I expect that future developments in information technology and communication (IT&C) will change and transform even more the way of operating in my area of responsibility

- strongly disagree
- disagree
- neutral
- agree
- strongly agree

0; 0%
0; 0%
4; 4%
32; 35%
57; 61%

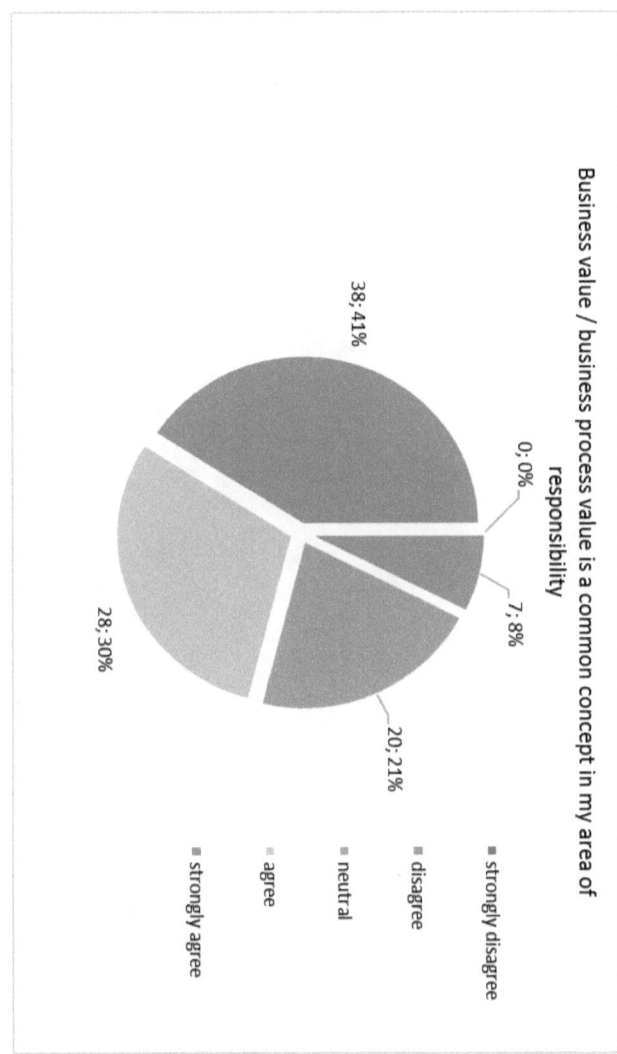

Business value / business process value is a common concept in my area of responsibility

- strongly disagree
- disagree
- neutral
- agree
- strongly agree

0; 0%
7; 8%
20; 21%
28; 30%
38; 41%

Item 9

Item 10

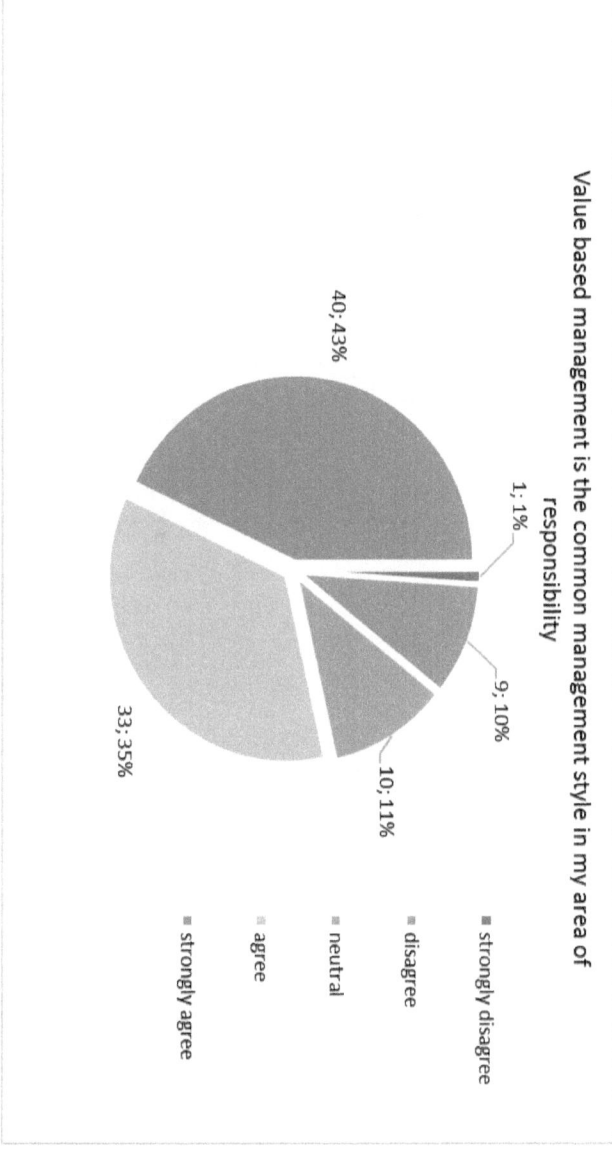

Value based management is the common management style in my area of responsibility

- strongly disagree
- disagree
- neutral
- agree
- strongly agree

1; 1%
9; 10%
10; 11%
33; 35%
40; 43%

Item 11

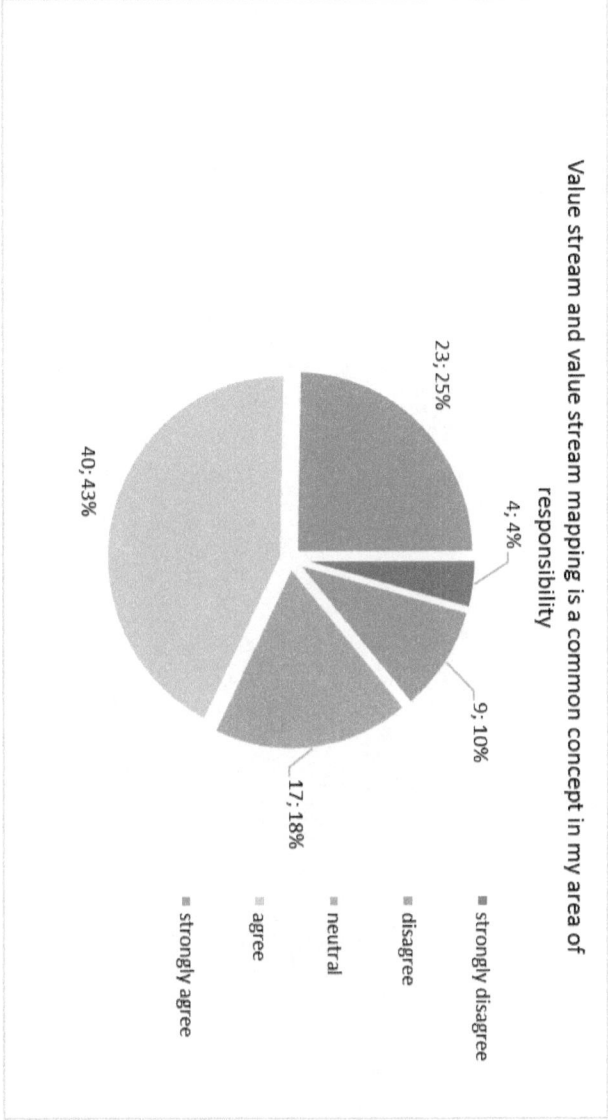

Value stream and value stream mapping is a common concept in my area of responsibility

- strongly disagree
- disagree
- neutral
- agree
- strongly agree

4; 4%

9; 10%

17; 18%

40; 43%

23; 25%

Item 12

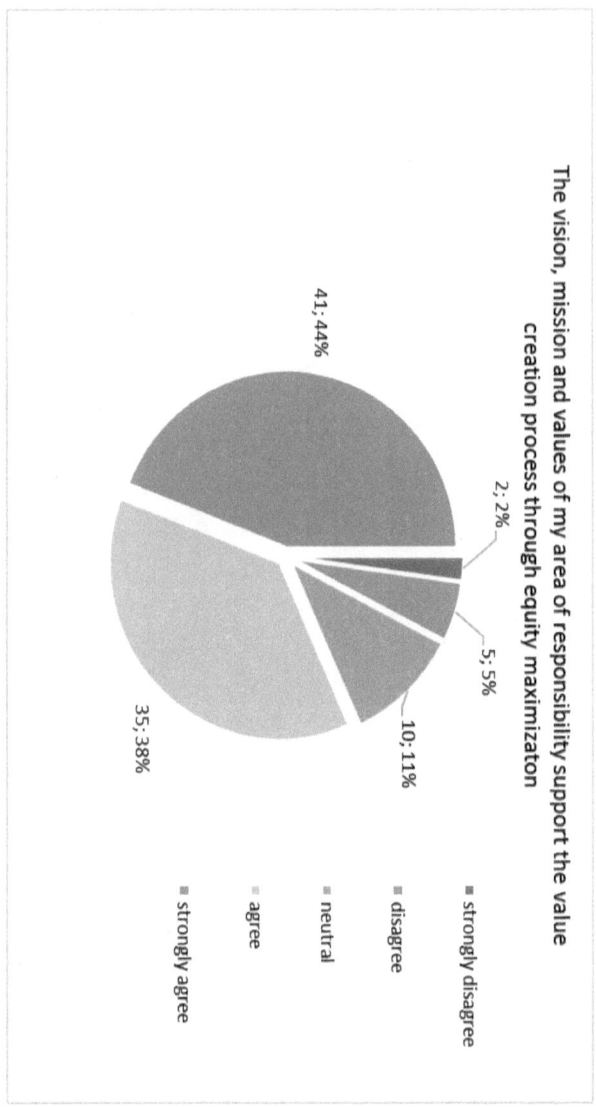

The vision, mission and values of my area of responsibility support the value creation process through equity maximizaton

- strongly disagree
- disagree
- neutral
- agree
- strongly agree

2; 2%
5; 5%
10; 11%
35; 38%
41; 44%

Item 13

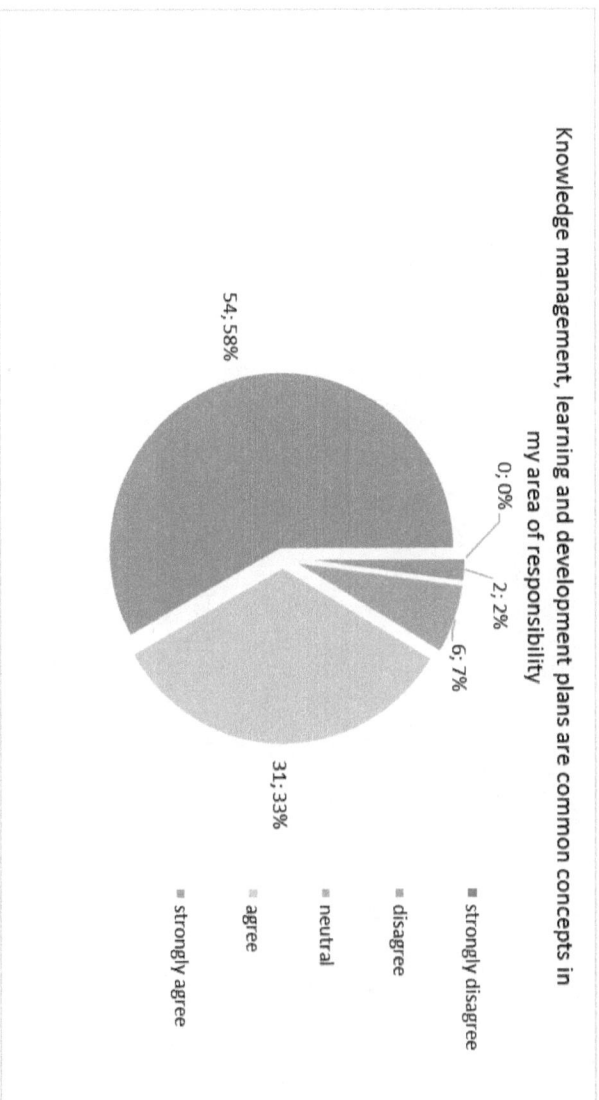

Knowledge management, learning and development plans are common concepts in my area of responsibility

- strongly disagree
- disagree
- neutral
- agree
- strongly agree

0; 0%
2; 2%
6; 7%
31; 33%
54; 58%

Item 14

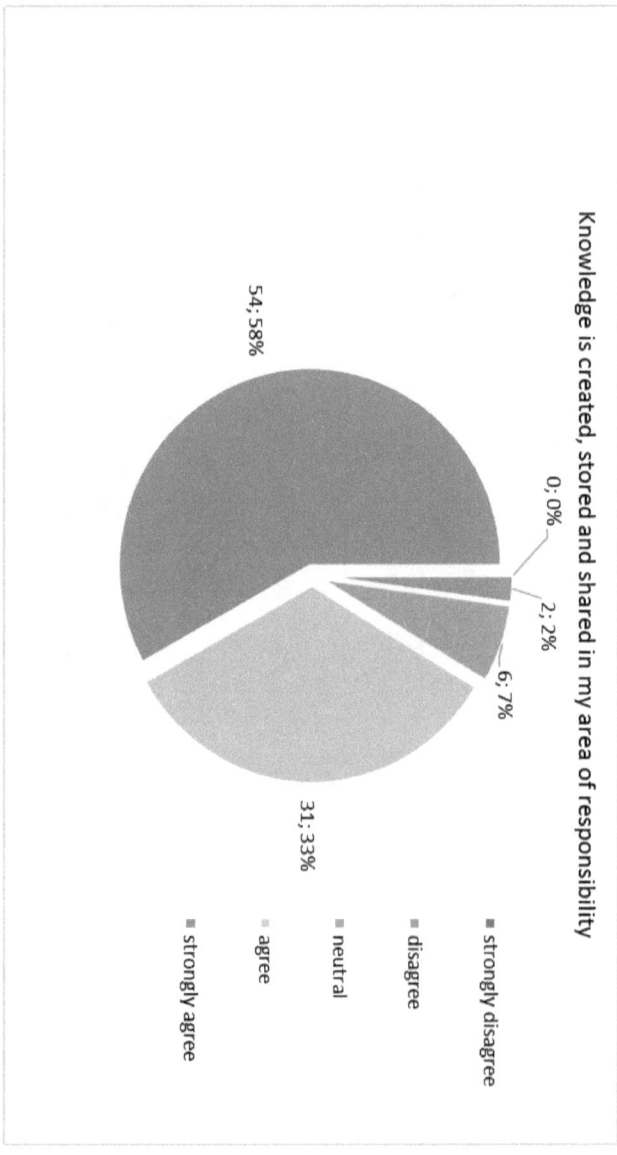

Knowledge is created, stored and shared in my area of responsibility

- strongly disagree
- disagree
- neutral
- agree
- strongly agree

0; 0%
2; 2%
6; 7%
31; 33%
54; 58%

Item 15

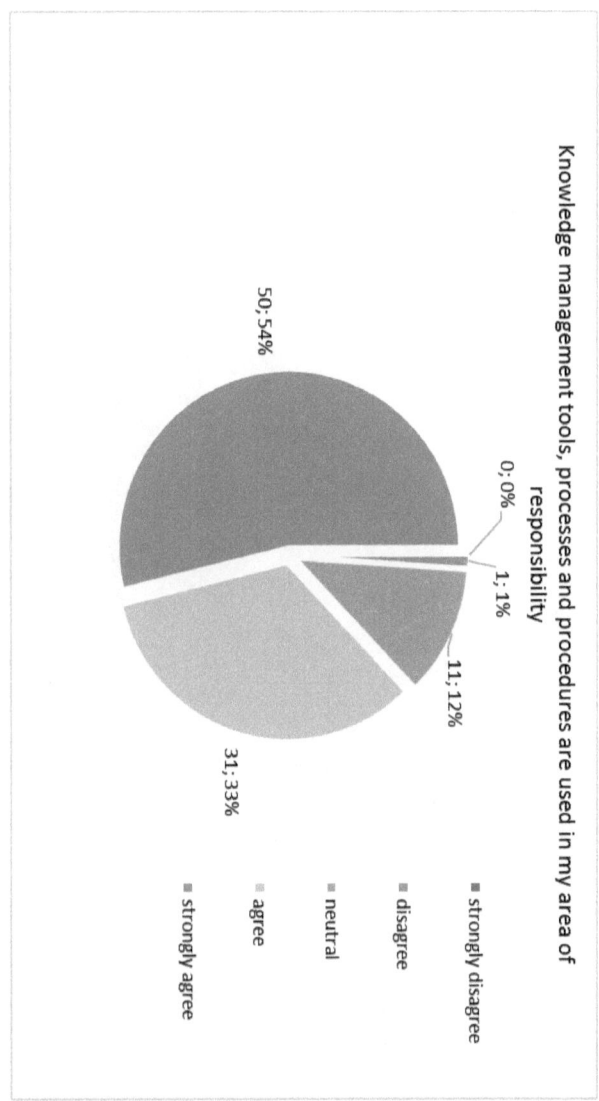

Knowledge management tools, processes and procedures are used in my area of responsibility

- strongly disagree
- disagree
- neutral
- agree
- strongly agree

0; 0%
1; 1%
11; 12%
31; 33%
50; 54%

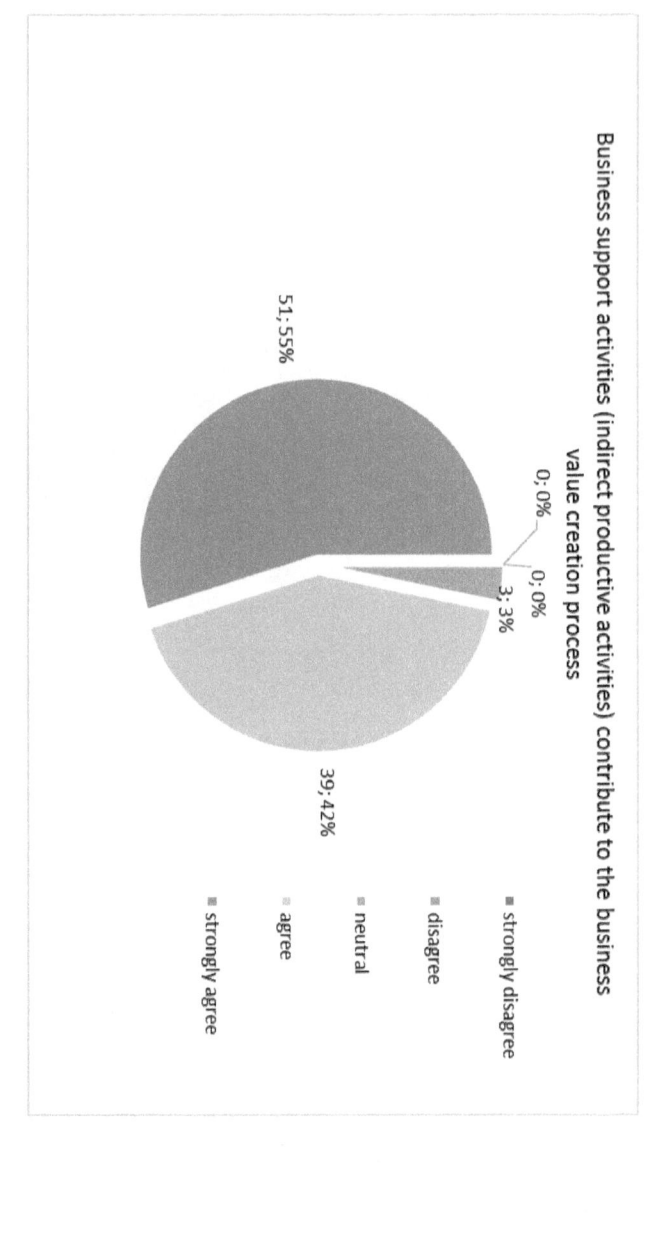

Business support activities (indirect productive activities) contribute to the business value creation process

0; 0%
0; 0%
3; 3%
51; 55%
39; 42%

- strongly disagree
- disagree
- neutral
- agree
- strongly agree

Item 16

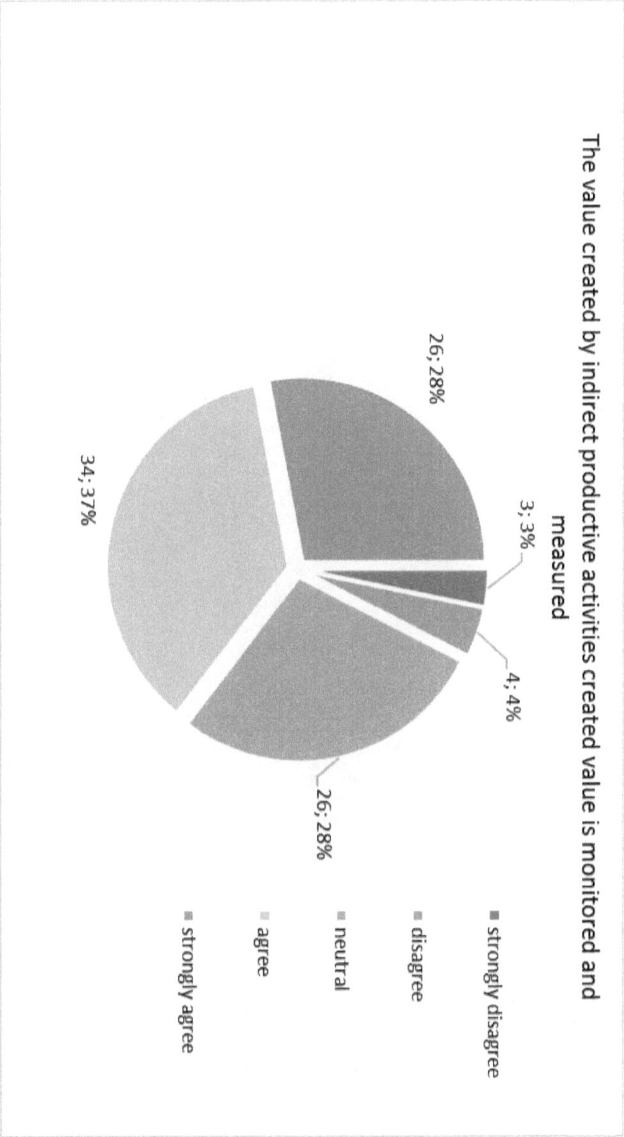

Item 17

The value created by indirect productive activities created value is monitored and measured

- strongly disagree
- disagree
- neutral
- agree
- strongly agree

3; 3%

4; 4%

26; 28%

26; 28%

34; 37%

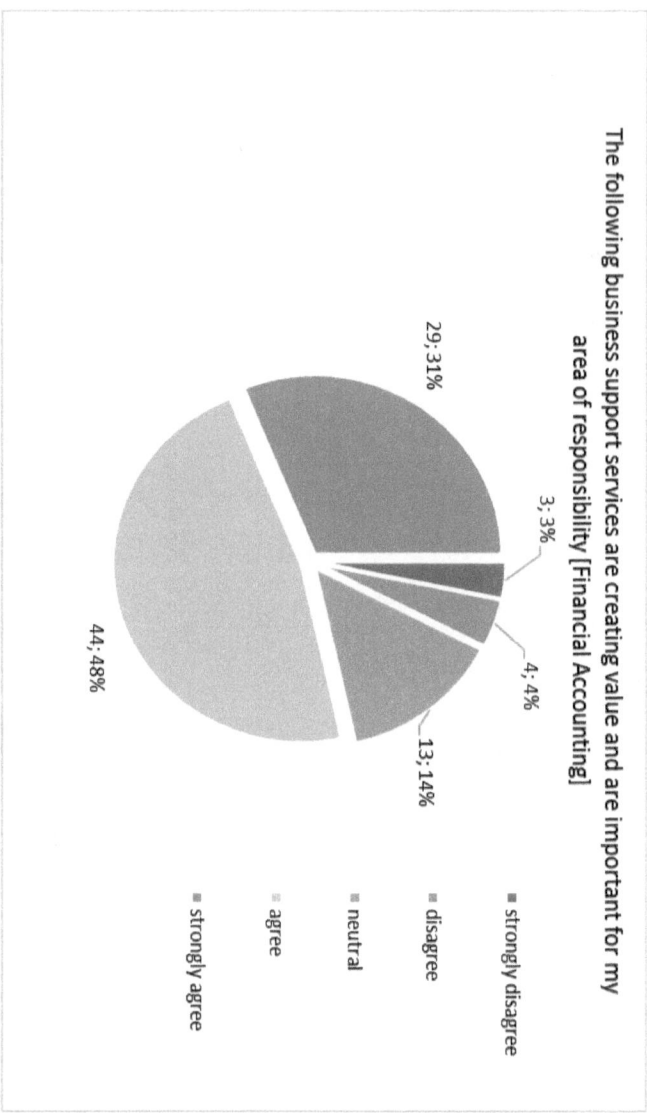

The following business support services are creating value and are important for my area of responsibility [Financial Accounting]

- strongly disagree
- disagree
- neutral
- agree
- strongly agree

3; 3%

4; 4%

13; 14%

29; 31%

44; 48%

Item 18

Item 19

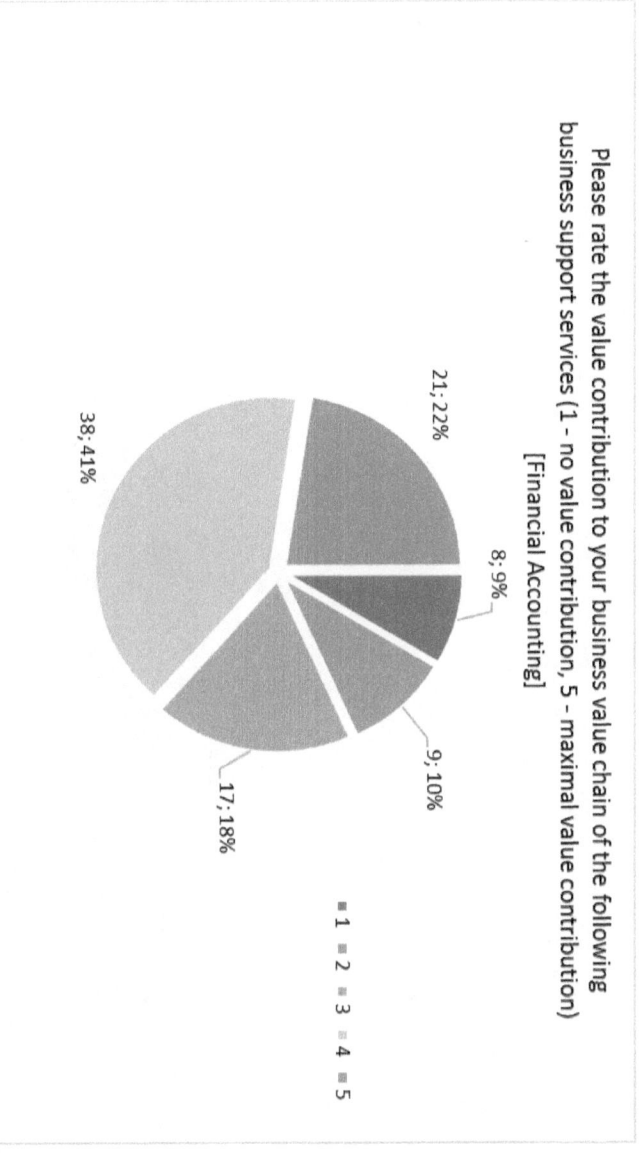

Please rate the value contribution to your business value chain of the following business support services (1 - no value contribution, 5 - maximal value contribution) [Financial Accounting]

21; 22%

8; 9%

9; 10%

17; 18%

38; 41%

■ 1 ■ 2 ■ 3 ■ 4 ■ 5

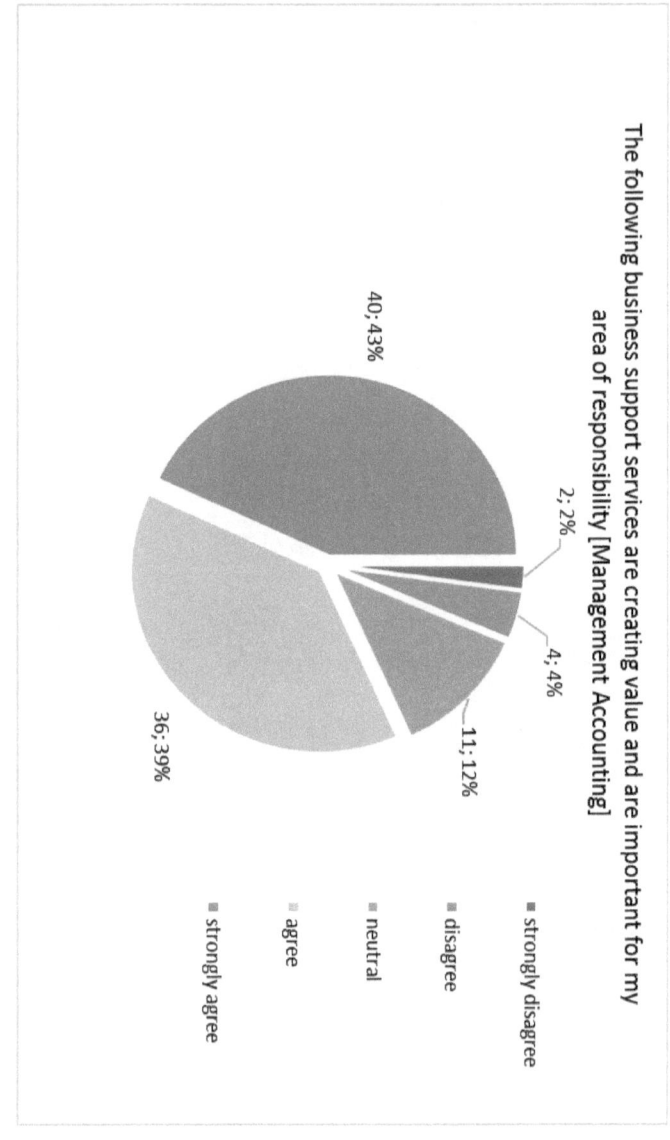

The following business support services are creating value and are important for my area of responsibility [Management Accounting]

- strongly disagree
- disagree
- neutral
- agree
- strongly agree

2; 2%
4; 4%
11; 12%
36; 39%
40; 43%

Item 20

Item 21

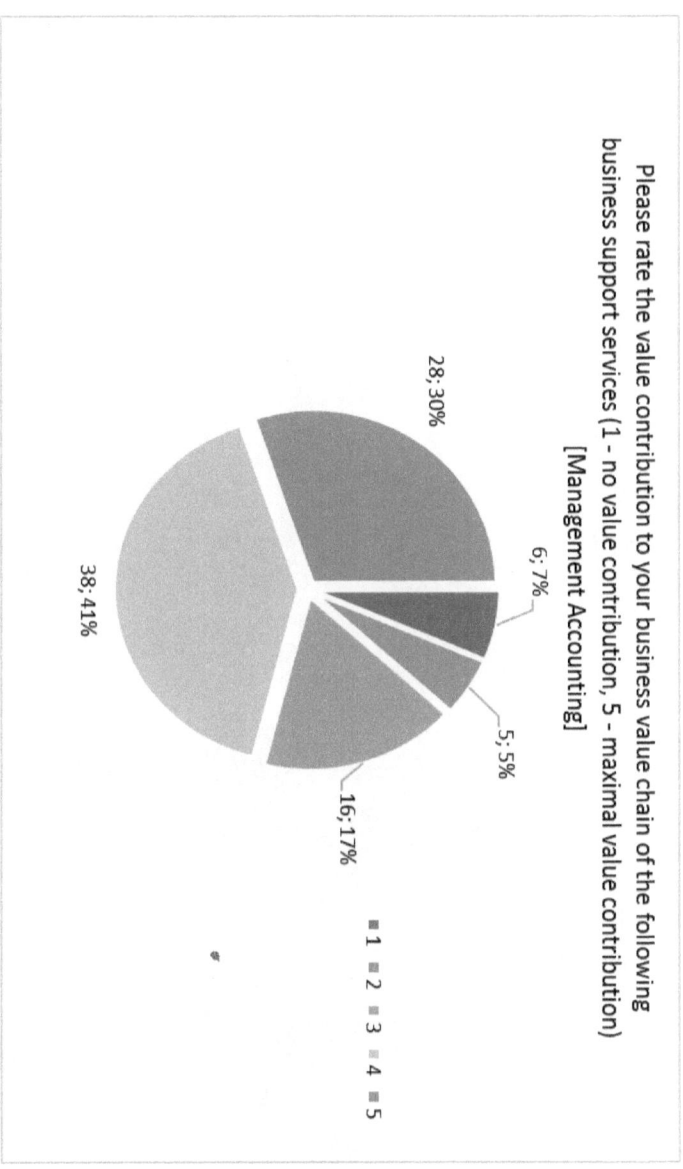

Please rate the value contribution to your business value chain of the following business support services (1 - no value contribution, 5 - maximal value contribution) [Management Accounting]

28; 30%

6; 7%

5; 5%

16; 17%

38; 41%

■ 1 ■ 2 ■ 3 ■ 4 ■ 5

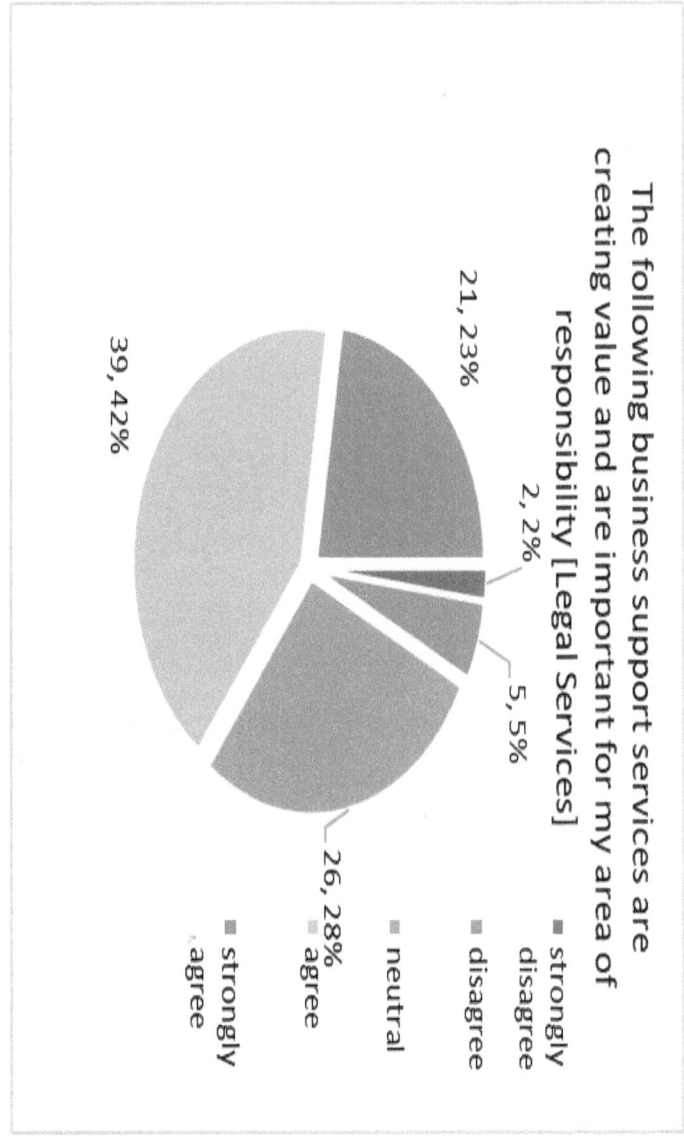

Item 22

Item 23

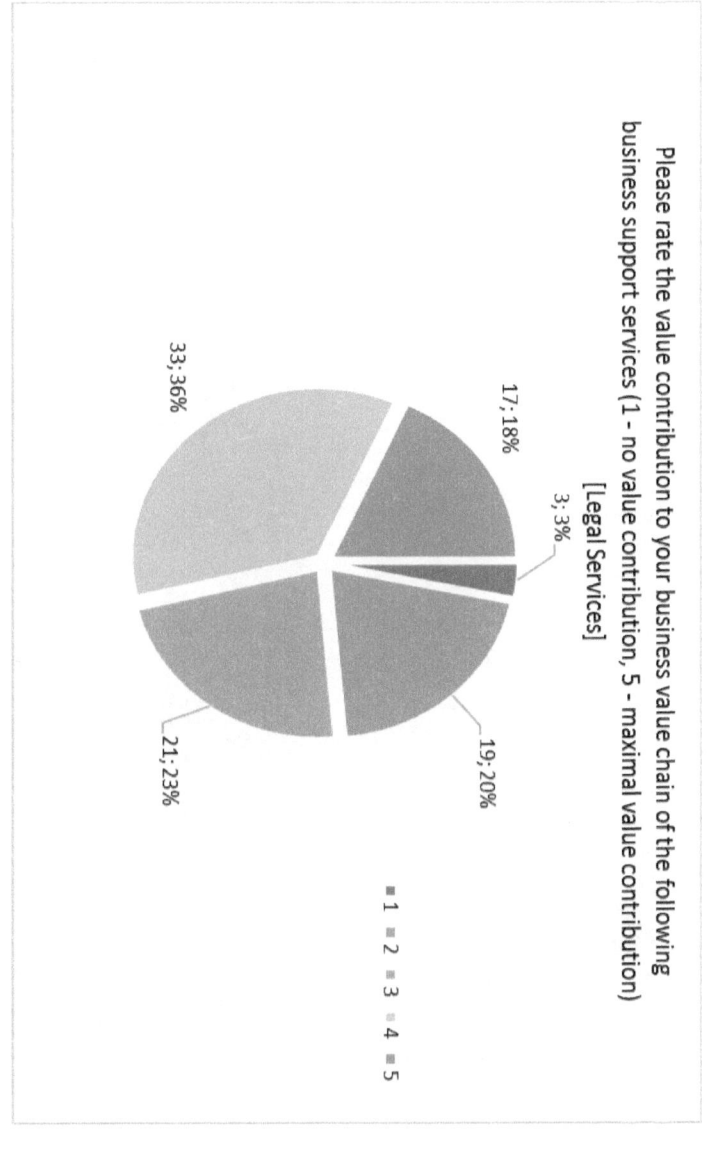

Please rate the value contribution to your business value chain of the following business support services (1 - no value contribution, 5 - maximal value contribution) [Legal Services]

3; 3%

17; 18%

19; 20%

21; 23%

33; 36%

■ 1 ■ 2 ■ 3 ■ 4 ■ 5

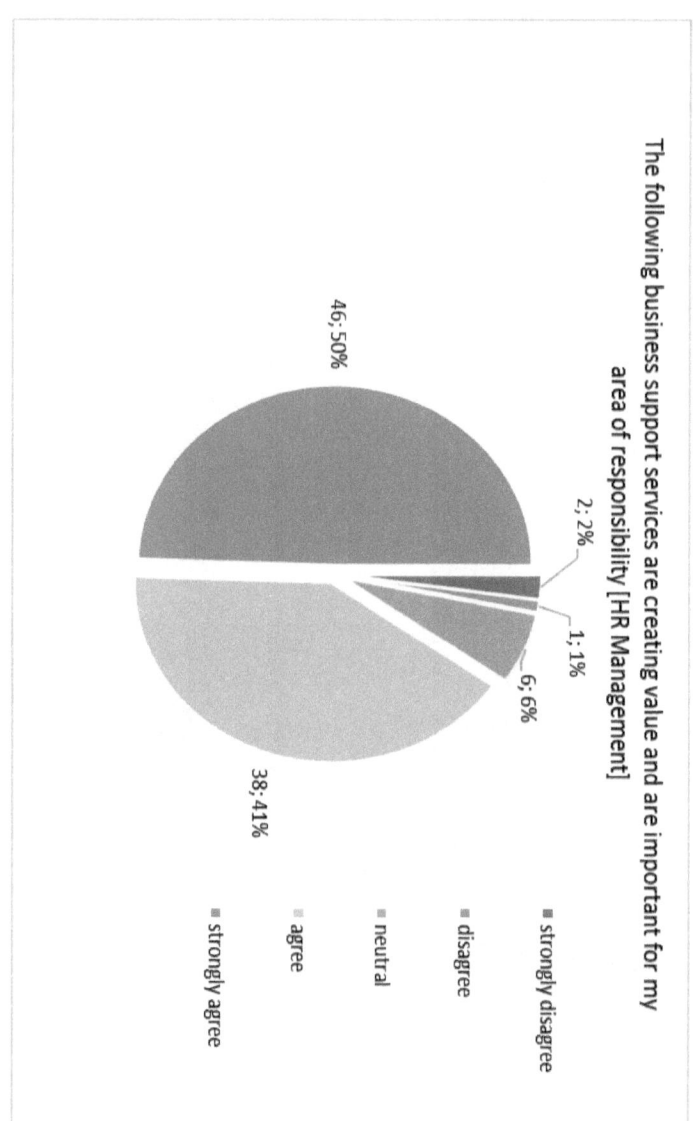

The following business support services are creating value and are important for my area of responsibility [HR Management]

- strongly disagree
- disagree
- neutral
- agree
- strongly agree

2; 2%
1; 1%
6; 6%
46; 50%
38; 41%

Item 24

Item 25

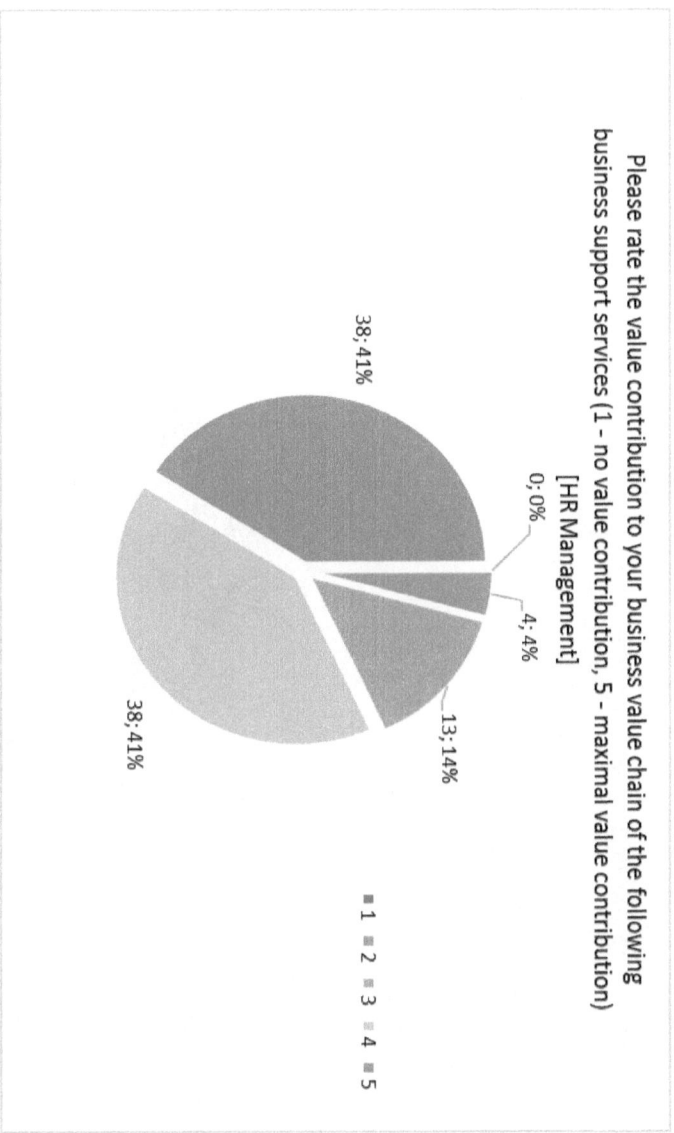

Please rate the value contribution to your business value chain of the following business support services (1 - no value contribution, 5 - maximal value contribution)
[HR Management]

0; 0%
4; 4%
13; 14%
38; 41%
38; 41%

■ 1 ■ 2 ■ 3 ■ 4 ■ 5

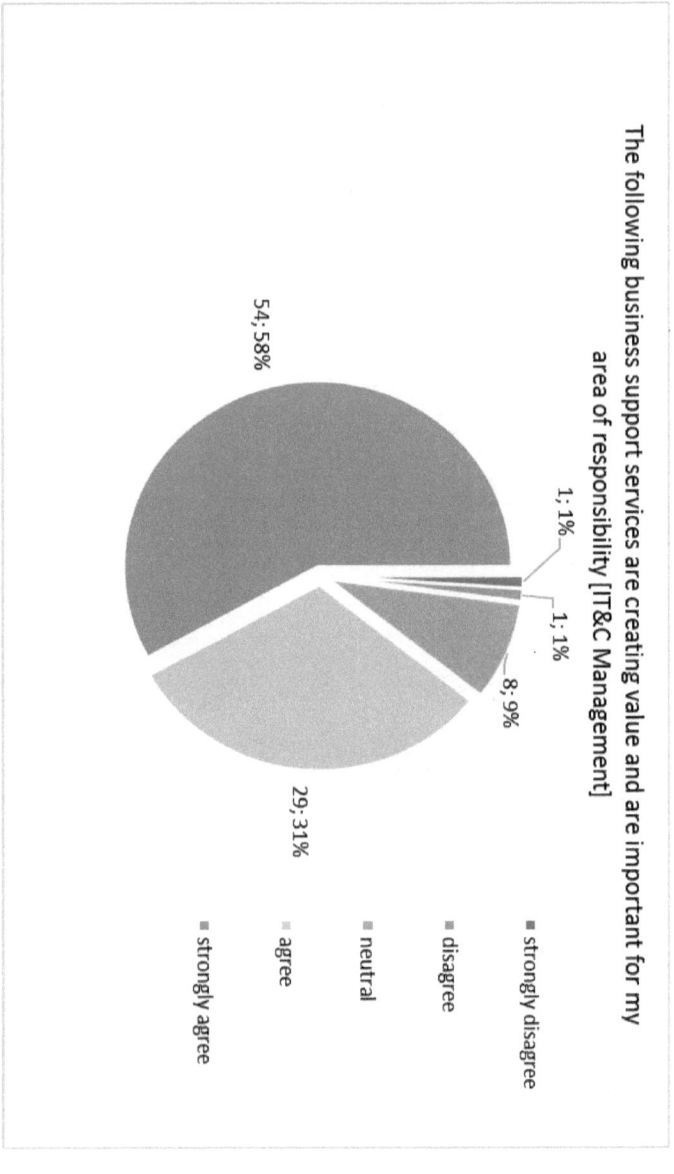

The following business support services are creating value and are important for my area of responsibility [IT&C Management]

- strongly disagree
- disagree
- neutral
- agree
- strongly agree

1; 1%
1; 1%
8; 9%
29; 31%
54; 58%

Item 26

Item 27

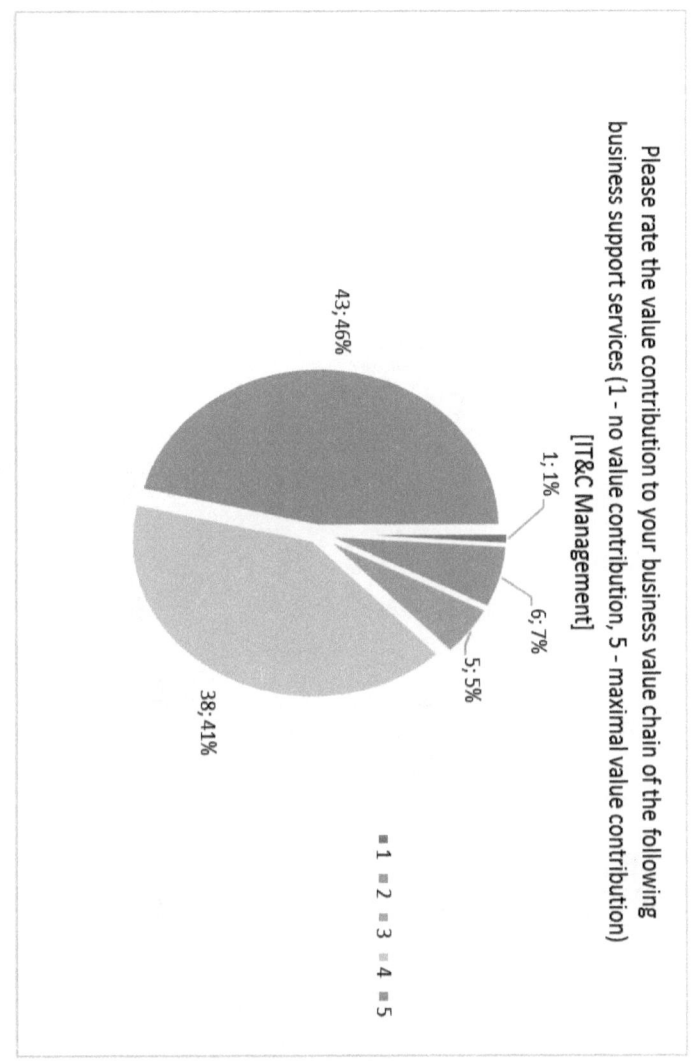

Please rate the value contribution to your business value chain of the following business support services (1 - no value contribution, 5 - maximal value contribution) [IT&C Management]

1; 1%

6; 7%

5; 5%

38; 41%

43; 46%

■ 1  ■ 2  ■ 3  ■ 4  ■ 5

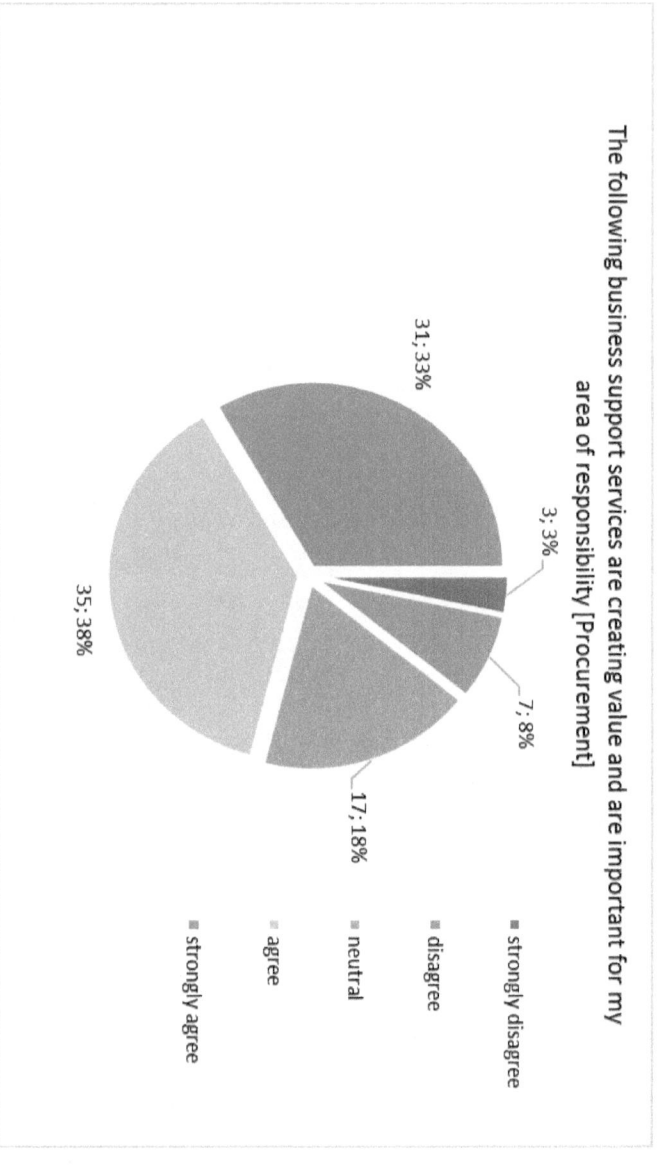

The following business support services are creating value and are important for my area of responsibility [Procurement]

- strongly disagree
- disagree
- neutral
- agree
- strongly agree

3; 3%

7; 8%

17; 18%

31; 33%

35; 38%

Item 28

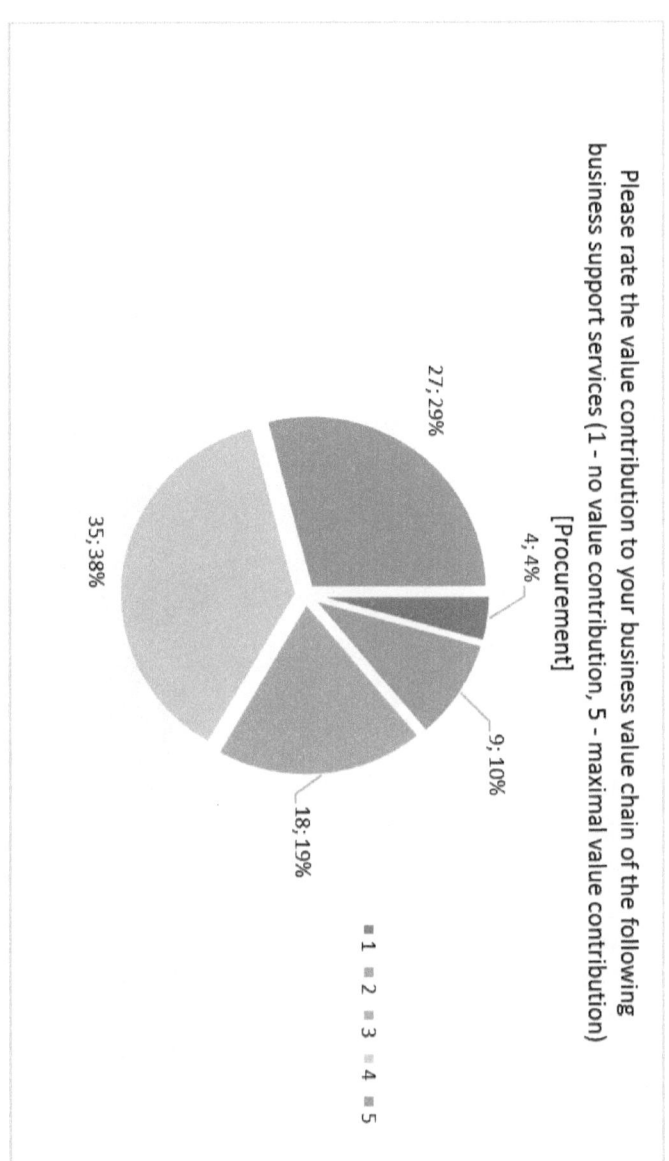

Please rate the value contribution to your business value chain of the following business support services (1 - no value contribution, 5 - maximal value contribution) [Procurement]

Item 29

Item 30

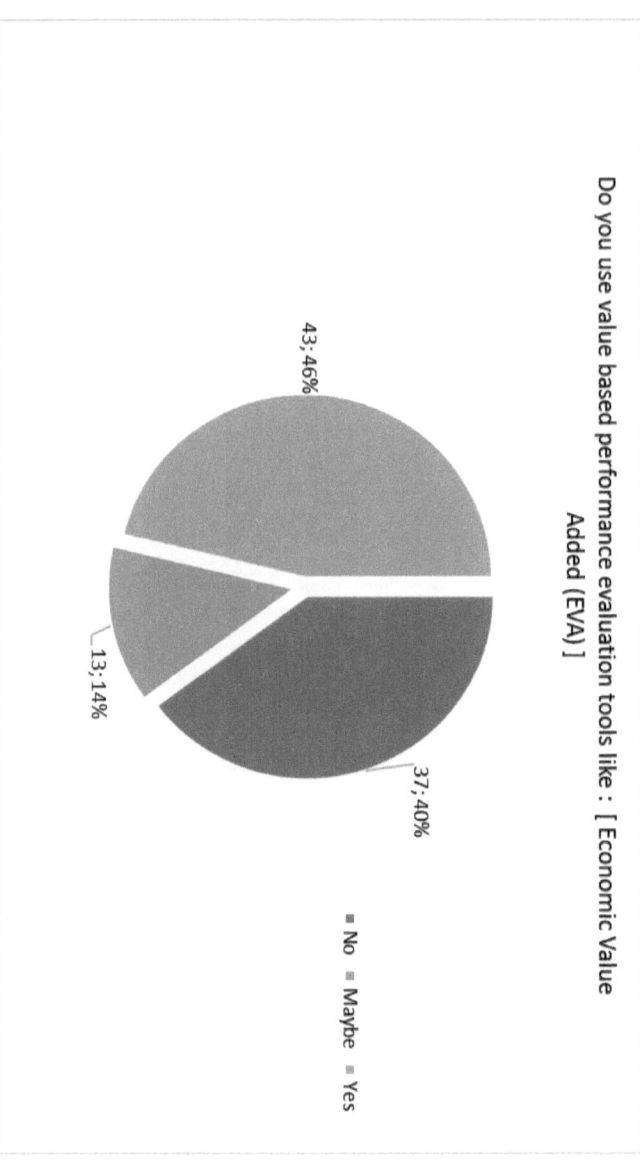

Do you use value based performance evaluation tools like : [ Economic Value Added (EVA) ]

43; 46%

13; 14%

37; 40%

■ No ■ Maybe ■ Yes

Item 31

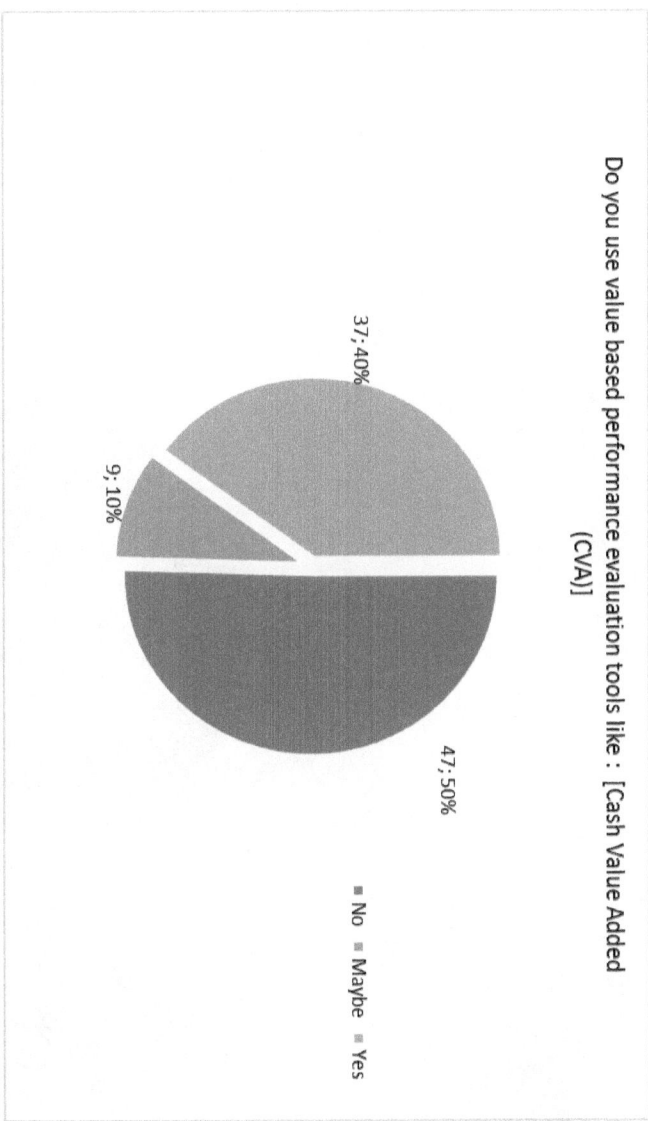

Do you use value based performance evaluation tools like : [Cash Value Added (CVA)]

37; 40%

9; 10%

47; 50%

■ No ■ Maybe ■ Yes

Item 32

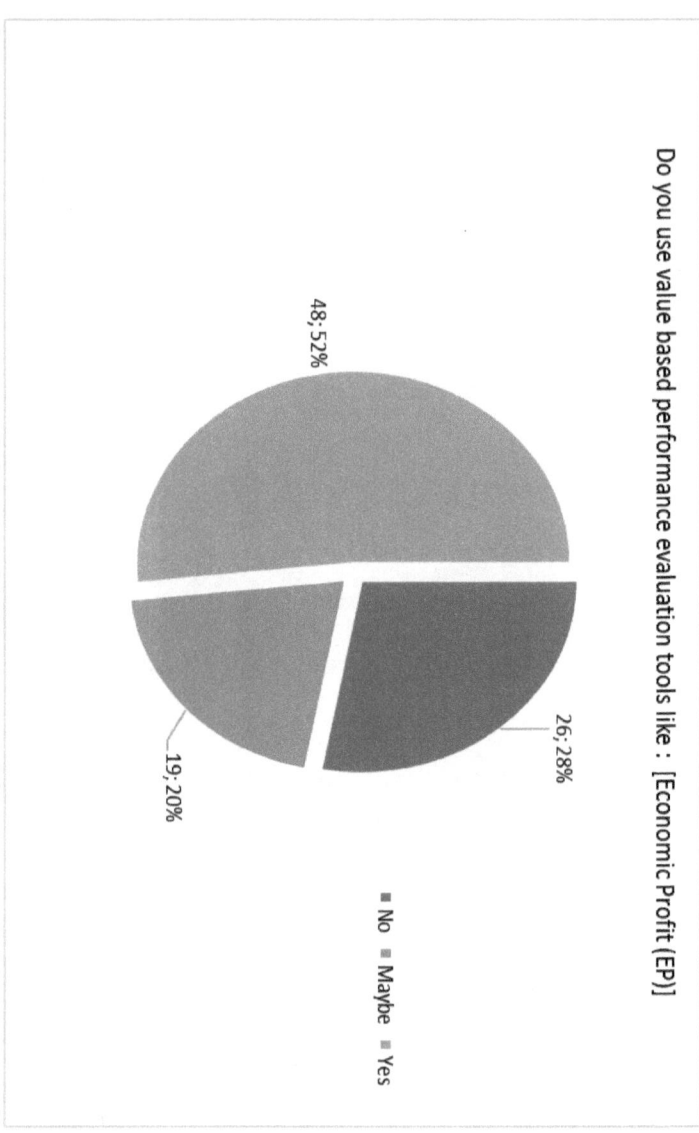

Do you use value based performance evaluation tools like : [Economic Profit (EP)]

48; 52%

26; 28%

19; 20%

■ No ■ Maybe ■ Yes

Item 33

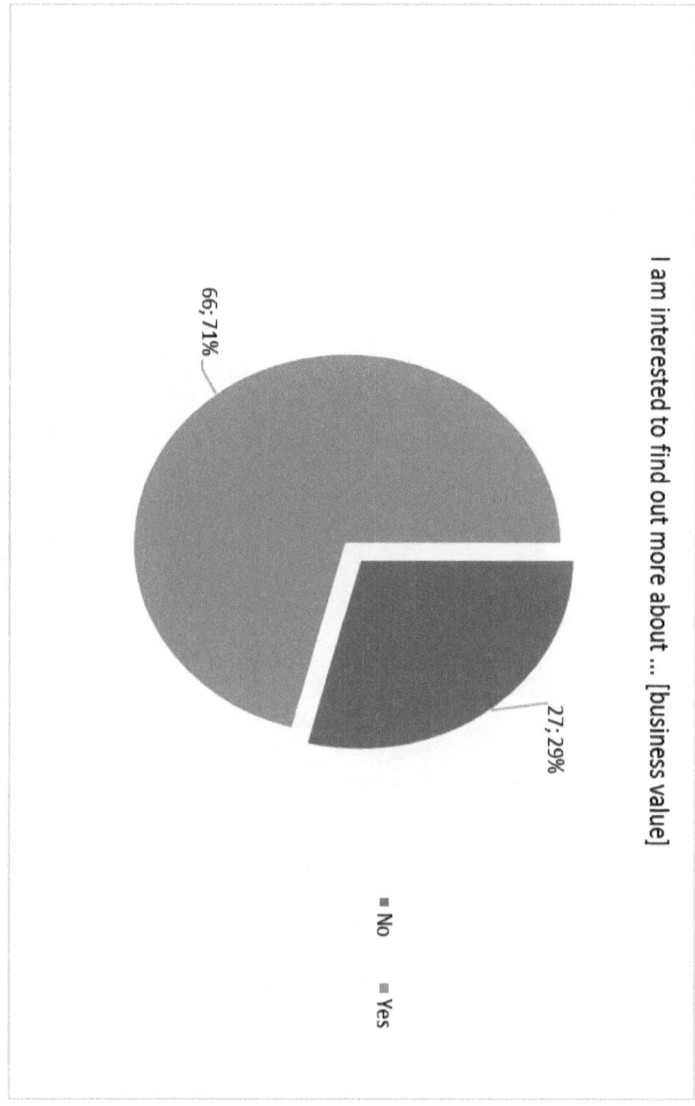

I am interested to find out more about ... [business value]

66; 71%

27; 29%

■ No

■ Yes

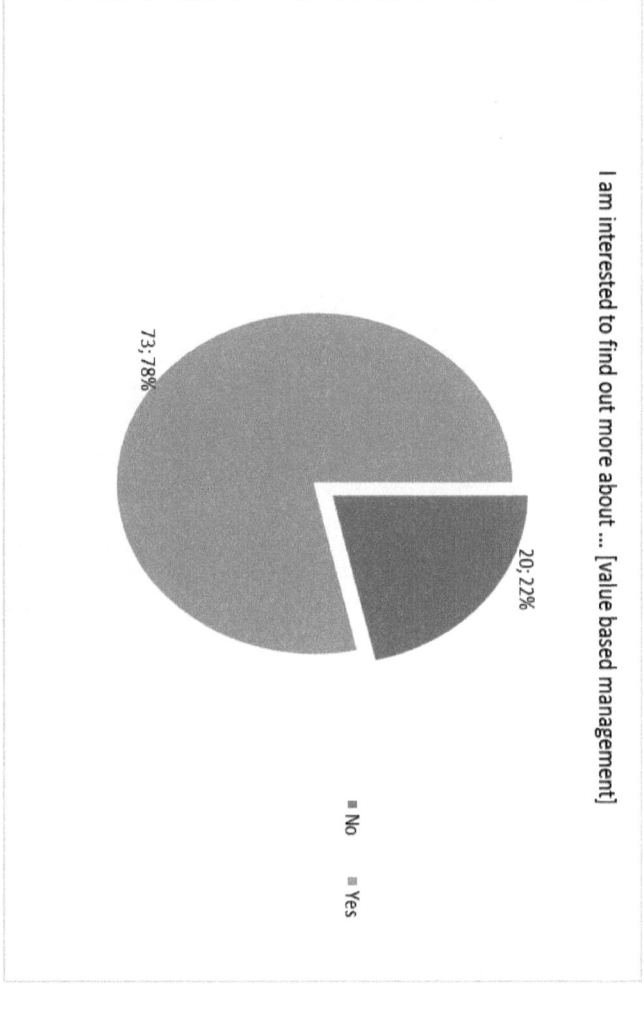

I am interested to find out more about ... [value based management]

73; 78%

20; 22%

■ No    ■ Yes

Item 34

I am interested to find out more about ... [Value based KPI's]

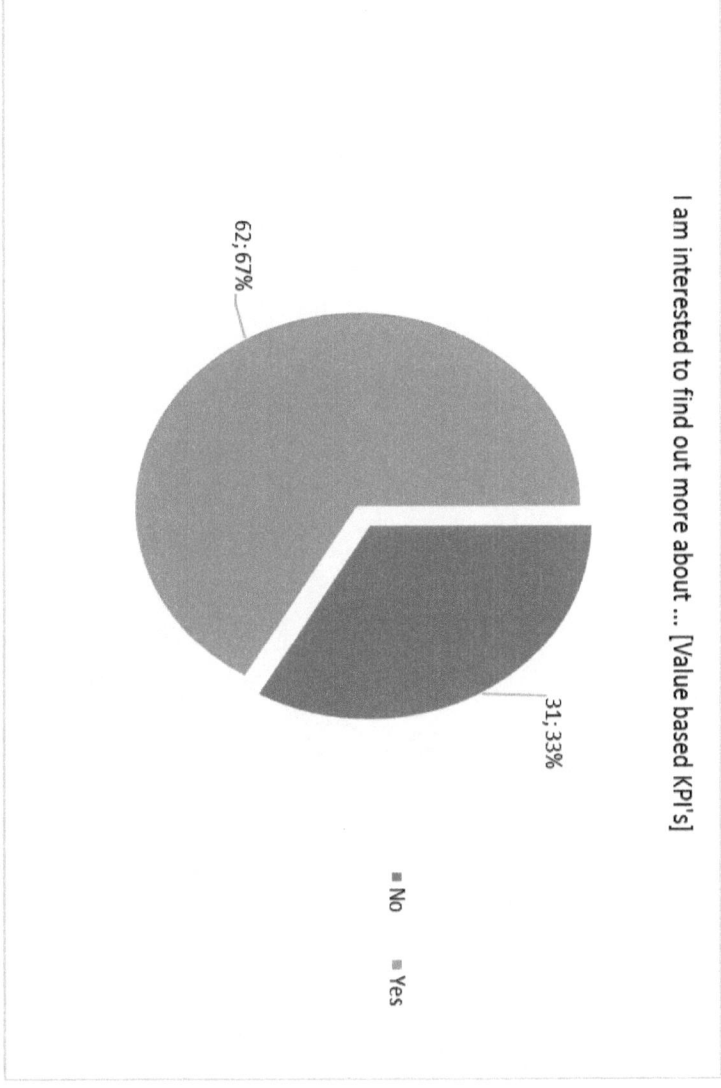

62; 67%

31; 33%

■ No ■ Yes

www.ingramcontent.com/pod-product-compliance
Lightning Source LLC
Chambersburg PA
CBHW030705220526
45463CB00005B/1909